BIG BOOK OF
FAVORITE CROCHET PATTERNS

EDITED BY

MARY CAROLYN WALDREP

DOVER PUBLICATIONS, INC., NEW YORK

Published in Canada by General Publishing Company, Ltd., 30 Lesmill Road, Don Mills, Toronto, Ontario.
Published in the United Kingdom by Constable and Company, Ltd., 3 The Lanchesters, 162–164 Fulham Palace Road, London W6 9ER.

This Dover edition, first published in 1991, is a new selection of patterns from *Crochet for Your Home, Book 67*, published by The Spool Cotton Company, New York, 1935; *Home Decoration, Book 76*, published by The Spool Cotton Company, 1936; *A Bookful of New Edgings, Book 109*, published by The Spool Cotton Company, 1937; *New Ideas in Crochet, Table Topics, Book No. 123*, published by The Spool Cotton Company, 1938; *Doilies, Luncheon Sets, Table Runners, Book No. 147*, published by The Spool Cotton Company, 1940; *Table Treasures, Book No. 152*, published by The Spool Cotton Company, 1940; *The Magic of Crochet, Book No. 168*, published by The Spool Cotton Company, 1941; *Crocheted Tablecloths and Luncheon Sets, Book No. 179*, published by The Spool Cotton Company, 1942; *New Table Topics, Book No. 185*, published by The Spool Cotton Company, 1942; *Bedspreads to Knit and Crochet, Book No. 186*, published by The Spool Cotton Company, 1942; *Filet Crochet, Book No. 193*, published by The Spool Cotton Company, 1943; *Laces and Edgings, Book No. 199*, published by The Spool Cotton Company, 1943; *Correct Table Settings, Book No. 260*, published by The Spool Cotton Company, 1949; *Priscilla Centerpieces, Book No. 276*, published by The Spool Cotton Company, 1951; *Old and New Favorites, Book No. 308*, published by Coats & Clark Inc., New York, 1954; *Priscilla Doilies to Crochet, Book No. 324*, published by Coats & Clark Inc., 1956; *Star Variety Show of Knitted and Crocheted Models, Star Book 21*, published by the American Thread Company, New York, 1942; *Star Book of Doilies, Book 22*, published by the American Thread Company, n.d.; *Conserve with Crochet . . . for the Home, Star Book No. 25*, published by the American Thread Company, n.d.; *Tatted & Crochet Designs, Star Book 30*, published by the American Thread Company, 1944; *Star Bedspreads, Book No. 34*, published by the American Thread Company, 1944; *Doilies, Star Book No. 44*, published by the American Thread Company, n.d.; *New Table Designs, Star Book No. 49*, published by the American Thread Company, 1946; *New Tablecloths, Star Book No. 57*, published by the American Thread Company, 1948; *Spreads That are Different in Motifs Easy to Make, Star Book No. 68*, published by the American Thread Company, 1949; *Doily Book, Star Doily Book No. 137*, published by the American Thread Company, n.d.; *Gifts, Novelties & Toys, Design Book No. 23*, published by the Lily Mills Company, Shelby, North Carolina, 1949; *Crochet & Tatted Edgings, Book No. 700-E*, published by the Lily Mills Company, n.d.; *Doilies, Design Book No. 67*, published by the Lily Mills Company, n.d.; *Crocheted Bedspreads, Book 900*, published by the Lily Mills Company, n.d.; *Doilies to Treasure, Book 1600*, published by the Lily Mills Company, n.d.; *Crochet for Today, Tomorrow and Always, Lily Direction Book 1700*, published by the Lily Mills Company, 1947; *Bucilla Cotton Crochet Creations, Vol. 117*, published by the Bernhard Ulmann Company, Inc., 1937; *Hand Crochet Decorations, Vol. 119*, published by the Bernhard Ulmann Company, Inc., 1937; *Bucilla Cotton Crochet, Vol. 121*, published by the Bernhard Ulmann Company, Inc., 1938; *Hand Crochet by Royal Society: Laces and Doilies, Book No. 3*, published by Royal Society, Inc., New York, 1943; and *Crocheted Bedspreads and Other Articles for the Home*, published by Sears, Roebuck and Company, n.d. A new Introduction has been written specially for this edition.

Manufactured in the United States of America
Dover Publications, Inc., 31 East 2nd Street, Mineola, N.Y. 11501

Library of Congress Cataloging-in-Publication Data

Big book of favorite crochet patterns / edited by Mary Carolyn Waldrep.
     p.   cm.
    ISBN 0-486-26359-2
    1. Crocheting—Patterns. I. Waldrep, Mary Carolyn.
TT820.B64 1991
746.43'4041—dc20

90-44919
CIP

Table of Contents

CROCHET ABBREVIATIONS

bal	balance	rnd	round
bl OR blk	block	rpt	repeat
ch	chain	sc	single crochet
dc	double crochet	s dc	short double crochet
dec	decrease	sk	skip
d tr	double treble	sl st	slip stitch
h dc	half double crochet	sp	space
inc	increase	st(s)	stitch(es)
incl	inclusive	tog	together
lp	loop	tr OR trc	treble crochet
p	picot	tr tr	triple treble (yarn over hook 4 times)
pc st	popcorn stitch		

* (asterisk) or † (dagger) . . . Repeat the instructions following the asterisk or dagger as many times as specified.

** or †† . . . Used for a second set of repeats within one set of instructions.

Repeat instructions in parentheses as many times as specified. For example: "**(Ch 5, sc in next sc) 5 times**" means to work all that is in parentheses 5 times.

STITCH CONVERSION CHART

U.S. Name	Equivalent
Chain	Chain
Slip	Single crochet
Single crochet	Double crochet
Half-double or short-double crochet	Half-treble crochet
Double crochet	Treble crochet
Treble crochet	Double-treble crochet
Double-treble crochet	Treble-treble crochet
Treble-treble or long-treble crochet	Quadruple-treble crochet
Afghan stitch	Tricot crochet

STEEL CROCHET HOOK CONVERSION CHART

U.S. Size	00	0	1	2	3	4	5	6	7	8	9	10	11	12	13	14
British & Canadian Size	000	00	0	1	–	1½	2	2½	–	3	–	4	–	5	–	6
Metric Size (mm)	3.00	2.75	2.50	2.25	2.10	2.00	1.90	1.80	1.65	1.50	1.40	1.25	1.10	1.00	0.75	0.60

Introduction

Although fashions in decoration come and go, the desire to create something beautiful for your home never goes out of style. During the first half of the twentieth century, hand-crocheted lace played an important role in fulfilling that desire. America's thread manufacturers produced a flood of instructional leaflets filled with bedspreads, tablecloths, doilies, edgings and other decorative accessories. Today, fine crochet is popular once again, and these old leaflets have become collector's items. The patterns in this book, collected from such leaflets, reflect some of the finest designs of the period.

All of the items in the book can be made with simple cotton crochet thread. Although the specific threads called for in the directions may be unavailable, other suitable threads can easily be found. Be careful in shopping for threads, however, since some product names used in the past are now being used on completely different threads. If you plan to use colored thread, be sure to buy enough at one time for the entire project, since colors can vary considerably from dye lot to dye lot.

While many of the patterns in the book list a gauge, others do not. A slight variation in the size of a doily or placemat is not significant, so do not let this trouble you. A gauge is rarely given for edgings, since they can be made in a variety of sizes. Whether or not the pattern lists a gauge, you should work a sample of the design, with the thread and hook suggested, before beginning the project. Check the appearance of your work—the stitches should be neat and firm, but not crowded. Compare your work to the gauge if one is given. If the piece is too small, use a larger hook; if it is too big, use a smaller hook.

When your project is complete, wash it in cool water using a mild soap. Squeeze the suds through the piece without rubbing, then rinse thoroughly. Using rustproof pins, pin the work, right side down, on a padded surface, pinning each picot and loop in place. When the piece is almost dry, press it through a damp cloth with a moderately hot iron. Do not allow the iron to rest on the stitches.

For larger pieces, such as bedspreads and tablecloths, that are made by sewing motifs together, you may find it easier to wash and block the individual motifs before joining them.

Doilies can be starched to give them a crisper look. Mix the starch following the manufacturer's directions and immerse the crocheted piece in the solution, squeezing it through the stitches. Squeeze out the excess and pin the doily to shape as described above.

The terminology and hooks listed in this book are those used in the United States. The charts opposite give the U.S. names of crochet stitches and their equivalents in other countries and the approximate equivalents to U.S. crochet hook sizes. Crocheters should become thoroughly familiar with the differences in both crochet terms and hook sizes before starting any project.

The stitches used in the projects in this book are explained on page 95. A metric conversion chart is located on page 96.

TABLECLOTHS AND PLACEMATS

Snow Crystal

Materials: Clark's O.N.T. (25 balls) or J. & P. Coats (17 balls) Mercerized Crochet, size 10, White or Ecru; or Clark's Big Ball Mercerized Crochet, size 10, 8 balls. Milward's steel crochet hook No. 8.

Continued on page 29

Formal
Buffet

72 x 110 Inches

MATERIALS: J. & P. Coats or Clark's O.N.T. Best Six Cord Mercerized Crochet, *Size 30:* **Small Ball:** J. & P. Coats—*16 balls of White or Ecru, or 21 balls of any color, or* Clark's O.N.T.—*24 balls of White or Ecru, or 30 balls of any color.* **Big Ball:** J. & P. Coats—*10 balls of White or Ecru, or 12 balls of any color . . . Steel Crochet Hook No. 10 . . . 7¼ yards of linen, 36 inches wide.*

GAUGE: 5 sps make 1 inch; 5 rows make 1 inch.

CROCHETED STRIP (Make 3) . . . Starting at one narrow end, make a chain 20 inches long (15 ch sts to 1 inch). **1st row:** Dc in 8th ch from hook (sp made), * ch 2, skip 2 ch, dc in next ch (another sp made). Repeat from * across until 74 sps in all are made. Cut off remaining chain. Ch 5, turn. **2nd row:** Skip first dc, dc in next dc (sp made over sp), ch 2, dc in next dc (another sp made over sp), make 12 more sps, 2 dc in next sp, dc in next dc (bl made over sp), make 3 more bls, 14 sps, 10 bls, 3 sps, 2 bls, 9 sps, 4 bls, 14 sps. Ch 5, turn. **3rd row:** Make 13 sps, 1 bl, ch 2, skip 2 dc, dc in next dc (sp made over bl), make 3 more sps, 1 bl, 10 sps, 1 bl, 2 sps, dc in next 3 dc (bl made over bl), make 3 more bls, 1 sp, 6 bls, 12 sps, 1 bl, 4 sps, 1 bl, 13 sps. Ch 5, turn.

Beginning with the 4th row on chart, follow chart to end. To complete strip, reverse chart and, omitting center row, follow chart back to beginning. Break off. Block pieces to measure 15 x 72 inches.

Cut 4 strips of linen 17 x 72½ inches. Make a narrow rolled hem all around outer edges of each piece. Whip crocheted strips between linen strips as in illustration.

EDGING . . . Starting at one narrow end, ch 8. **1st row:** Dc in 8th ch from hook. Ch 5, turn. **2nd row:** Skip 2 ch, dc in next ch. Ch 5, turn. **3rd row:** Skip 2 ch, dc in next ch. Ch 8, turn. **4th row:** Dc in next dc, ch 2, skip 2 ch, dc in next ch. Ch 5, turn. **5th and 6th rows:** Skip first dc, dc in next dc, ch 2, skip 2 ch, dc in next ch. Ch 5, turn. **7th row:** Skip first dc, dc in next dc. Ch 5, turn. Repeat 2nd to 7th rows incl until piece is long enough to go all around outer edges of cloth. Sc closely along scalloped edge of Edging. Whip Edging in place all around outer edges of cloth.

NAPKIN (Make 12) . . . Cut a piece of linen, 18 inches square. Make a narrow rolled hem all around outer edges. Make Edging as for Tablecloth. Whip Edging in place.

↑
CENTER ROW

11

Summer Snowflake

Airily enmeshed in filmy festoons, the snowflake motif asserts its crisp beauty.

MATERIALS: CLARK'S O.N.T. or J. & P. COATS
BEST SIX CORD MERCERIZED CROCHET, size 20:

SMALL BALL: BIG BALL:
CLARK'S O.N.T.—66 balls,   J. & P. COATS—22 balls.
      OR
J. & P. COATS—38 balls.

Steel crochet hook No. 8 or 9.   *Directions on page 30*

Ardmore

Directions on page 30

Afternoon Tea

Materials Required—AMERICAN THREAD COMPANY "STAR" SIX CORD MERCERIZED CROCHET COTTON, ARTICLE 77

7—250 Yd. Balls will make 4 Doilies.

Doily measures about 14 x 20 inches.

Steel Crochet Hook No. 12.

Ch 63, cluster st in 11th st from hook, (cluster st: thread over needle, insert in st and work off 2 loops, * thread over needle, insert in same space and work off 2 loops, repeat from *, thread over and work off all loops at one time) ch 3, skip 3 sts of ch, cluster st in next st, repeat from * across row ending row with ch 6, skip 3 sts of ch, sl st in 1st st of ch.

2nd Row. Ch 7, s c in same loop, ch 7, s c in same loop, then working around entire 1st row * ch 7, s c in next loop, repeat from * 11 times, ch 7, s c in end loop, * ch 7, s c in same loop, repeat from * 3 times, * ch 7, s c in next loop, repeat from * 11 times, ch 7, s c in end loop, ch 7, s c in same loop, ch 3, d c in same st with 1st ch 7. (This brings thread in position for next row.)

3rd Row. * Ch 7, s c in next loop, repeat from * all around ending row with ch 3, d c in d c.

4th Row. Ch 3, * thread over needle, insert in same space and work off 2 loops, repeat from *, thread over and work off all loops at one time, ch 5, 4 cluster sts with ch 5 between each cluster st in next loop. * ch 5, cluster st in next loop, repeat from * all around working 4 clusters sts with ch 5 between each cluster st in end loop and ending row with ch 3, d c in top of 1st cluster st.

5th Row. Ch 7, s c in next loop, ch 7, s c in next loop, ch 7, s c in same loop, ch 7, s c in next loop, * ch 7, s c in same loop, repeat from *, ch 7, s c in next loop, ch 7, s c in same loop, * ch 7, s c in next loop, repeat from * 17 times, ch 7, s c in same loop, ch 7, s c in next loop, * ch 7, s c in same loop, repeat from *, ch 7, s c in next loop, ch 7, s c in same loop, * ch 7, s c in next loop repeat from * 14 times, ch 3, d c in d c.

6th, 7th and 8th Rows. * Ch 7, s c in next loop, repeat from * all around ending each row with ch 3, d c in d c.

9th Row. Ch 3, cluster st in same loop, * ch 5, cluster st in next loop, repeat from * 4 times, ch 5, cluster st in same loop, ch 5, 2 cluster sts with ch 5 between in next loop, ch 5, 3 cluster sts with ch 5 between each cluster st in next loop, * ch 5, 2 cluster sts with ch 5 between in next loop, repeat from *, ch 5, cluster st in next loop, * ch 5, cluster st in next loop, repeat from * 18 times, ch 5, cluster st in same loop, ch 5, 2 cluster sts with ch 5 between in next loop, ch 5, 3 cluster sts with ch 5 between in next loop, * ch 5, 2 cluster sts with ch 5 between in next loop, repeat from *, * ch 5, cluster st in next loop, repeat from * across side ending row with ch 5, join in 1st cluster st.

10th Row. Sl st to loop, ch 3, cluster st in same space, * ch 5, cluster st in next loop, repeat from * all around, ch 5, join.

11th Row. Sl st to loop, ch 3, cluster st in same space, * ch 5, cluster st in next loop, repeat from *, * ch 5, 2 cluster sts with ch 5 between in next loop, ch 5, cluster st in next loop, repeat from * twice, ch 5, 3 cluster sts with ch 5 between each cluster st in next loop, * ch 5, cluster st in next loop, ch 5, 2 cluster sts with ch 5 between in next loop, repeat from * twice, * ch 5, cluster st in next loop, repeat from * 16 times, * ch 5, 2 cluster sts with ch 5 between in next loop, ch 5, cluster st in next loop, repeat from * twice, ch 5, 3 cluster sts with ch 5 between each cluster st in next loop, * ch 5, cluster st in next loop, ch 5, 2 cluster sts with ch 5 between in next loop, repeat from * twice, ch 5, cluster st in next loop, repeat from * 13 times, ch 3, d c in top of 1st cluster st.

12th Row. * Ch 7, s c in next loop, repeat from * all around ending row with ch 2, tr c in d c.

13th, 14th, 15th, 16th, 17th and 18th Rows. 2 s c in same space, * ch 7, 2 s c in next loop, repeat from * all around ending each row with ch 2, tr c in 1st s c.

19th Row. Ch 3, cluster st in same space, * ch 6, cluster st in next loop, repeat from * 7 times, * ch 6, 2 cluster sts with ch 6 between in next loop, ch 6, cluster st in next loop, repeat from * 3 times, ch 6, 3 cluster sts with ch 6 between each cluster st in next loop, * ch 6, cluster st in next loop, ch 6, 2 cluster sts with ch 6 between in next loop, repeat from * 3 times, * ch 6, cluster st in next loop, repeat from * 20 times, ch 6, 2 cluster sts with ch 6 between in next loop, then work end same as opposite end and work side to correspond, ch 6, join in 1st cluster st.

20th Row. Same as 10th row but having ch 6 between each cluster st.

21st Row. Sl st to loop, ch 3, cluster st in same space, * ch 6, cluster st in next loop, repeat from * 7 times, * ch 6, 2 cluster sts with ch 6 between in next loop, ch 6, cluster st in next loop, ch 6, cluster st in next loop, repeat from * 3 times, ch 6, 3 cluster sts with ch 6 between each cluster st in next loop, * ch 6, cluster st in next loop, ch 6, cluster st in next loop, ch 6, 2 cluster sts with ch 6 between in next loop, repeat from * 3 times, * ch 6, cluster st in next loop, repeat from * 22 times, ch 6, 2 cluster sts with ch 6 between in next loop, then work around end same as opposite end and work other side to correspond ending row with ch 3, d c in top of 1st cluster st.

22nd Row. Ch 8, s c in next loop, repeat from beginning all around ending row with ch 2, tr c in d c.

23rd, 24th, 25th, 26th, 27th and 28th Rows. 2 s c in same space, * ch 7, 2 s c in next loop, repeat from * all around ending each row with ch 2, tr c in 1st s c.

29th Row. Ch 3, cluster st in same space, * ch 7, cluster st in next loop, repeat from * 23 times, ch 7, 2 cluster sts with ch 7 between in next loop, * ch 7, cluster st in next loop, repeat from * 8 times, ch 7, 2 cluster sts with ch 7 between in next loop, * ch 7, cluster st in next loop, repeat from * 46 times, ch 7, 2 cluster sts with ch 7 between in next loop, * ch 7, cluster st in next loop, repeat from * 8 times, ch 7, 2 cluster sts with ch 7 between in next loop, then work 1 cluster st in each loop, with ch 7 between cluster sts, join in 1st cluster st (120 cluster sts).

Continued on page 17

To Love and Cherish

MATERIALS—Lily DAISY Mercerized Crochet Cotton, size 30:—22 skeins or balls White, Cream or Ecru. Crochet hook size 13. 108 blocks 9x12 are required for a tablecloth about 62x82 inches.

BLOCK—(Size 6½ inches when blocked)—Ch 9, sl st in starting st. Ch 3, 19 dc in ring, sl st in 1st 3-ch. **ROW 2**—Ch 3, (dc, ch 3, 2 dc) in same st, * ch 9, (2 dc, ch 3, 2 dc) in next 5th dc. Repeat from * twice. Ch 4, tr in 1st 3-ch. **ROW 3**—Ch 3, turn, (dc, ch 3, 2 dc) in tr, * ch 4, (3 dc, ch 3, 3 dc) in center of next shell, ch 4, (2 dc, ch 3, 2 dc) in 5th st of next 9-ch. Repeat from * around. End with 4-ch, sl st in top of 1st 3-ch, sl st in next dc, sl st in next sp. **ROW 4**—Ch 8, turn, * (3 dc, ch 3, 3 dc) in next shell, ch 5, 9 dc in next shell, ch 5 and repeat from * around. End with 8 dc, sl st in 3d st of 1st 8-ch. **ROW 5**—Ch 4, turn, dc in next dc, (ch 1, dc in next dc) 7 times, * ch 5, (3 dc, ch 3, 3 dc) in next shell, ch 5, dc in 1st dc of next pineapple, (ch 1, dc in next dc) 8 times. Repeat from * around. End with 5-ch, sl st in 3d st of 1st 4-ch. Sl st in next 1-ch sp. **ROW 6**—Turn, * ch 5, (2 dc, ch 3, 2 dc) in next shell, ch 5, sc in 1st 1-ch sp of pineapple, (ch 5, sc in next 1-ch sp) 7 times. Repeat from * around. End with six 5-ch lps, ch 2, dc in end 1-ch sp. **ROW 7**—

Turn, * (ch 5, sc in next lp) 6 times, ch 5, (3 dc, ch 3, 3 dc) in each of 2 sps in next shell, ch 5, sc in 1st 5-ch lp on next pineapple. Repeat from * around. End with 5-ch, sl st at start of row. Sl st to center of 1st lp. **ROW 8**—Turn, * ch 5, (3 dc, ch 3, 3 dc) in next shell, ch 7, sk 6 dc, a shell in next sp, ch 5, sc in 1st lp of pineapple, (ch 5, sc in next lp) 5 times. Repeat from * around. End with four 5-ch lps, ch 2, dc in next lp. **ROW 9**—Turn, * (ch 5, sc in next lp) 4 times, ch 5, a shell in next shell, ch 4, (tr, ch 7, tr) in 4th st of next 7-ch lp, ch 4, a shell in next shell, ch 5, sc in 1st lp of next pineapple. Repeat from * around. Sl st to center of next lp. **ROW 10**—Turn, * ch 5, a shell in next shell, ch 5, 3 dc in corner lp, (ch 3, 3 dc) 3 times in same lp, ch 5, a shell in next shell, ch 5, sc in 1st lp of pineapple. Repeat from * around. End with two 5-ch lps, ch 2, dc in next lp. **ROW 11**—Turn, * (ch 5, sc in next lp) twice, ch 5, a shell in next shell, ch 5, a shell in 1st sp on corner shell, (ch 1, a shell in next sp) twice, ch 5, a shell in next shell, ch 5, sc in 1st lp of pineapple. Repeat from * around. Sl st to center of 1st lp. **ROW 12**—Turn, * ch 5, a shell in next shell, ch 7, a shell in next shell, ch 5, (3 dc, ch 3, 3 dc, ch 3, 3 dc) in next shell, ch 5, a shell in next shell, ch 7, a shell in next shell, ch 5, sc in 1st lp on pineapple, ch 5, sc in next lp. Repeat from * around, making 2-ch and dc instead of final 5-ch lp. **ROW 13**—Turn, * ch 5, a shell in next shell, ch 9, a shell in next shell, ch 5, a shell in 1st sp of corner shell, ch 2, a shell in next sp, ch 5, a shell in next shell, ch 9, a shell in next shell, ch 5, sc in tip of pineapple. Repeat from * around. **ROW 14**—Turn, * ch 5, a shell in next shell, ch 11, a shell in next shell, ch 6, a shell in next shell, ch 7, sk corner sp, a shell in next shell, ch 7, a shell in next shell, ch 11, a shell in next shell, ch 5, sc in next sc. Repeat from * around. End with tr instead of final 5-ch. **ROW 15**—Turn, sl st to center sp of last shell, ch 3, (2 dc, ch 3, 3 dc) in same sp, * ch 13, a shell in next shell, ch 7, a shell in next shell, ch 3, (tr, ch 9, tr) in 4th st of corner lp, ch 3, a shell in next shell, ch 7, a shell in next shell, ch 13, a shell in next shell, a shell in next shell. Repeat from * around. End with sl st in 1st 3-ch, sl st to center sp of shell. **ROW 16**—Ch 3, turn, 2 dc in same sp, * ch 5, sl st in last dc for a p, 3 dc in next shell, ch 15, a shell in next shell, ch 7, a shell in next shell, ch 3, dc in next tr, (5 dc, a p and 5 dc) in next lp, dc in tr, ch 3, a shell in next shell, ch 7, a shell in next shell, ch 15, 3 dc in next shell. Repeat from * around. End with 15-ch, sl st in 1st 3-ch. Cut 6 inches long, thread to a needle and fasten off on back.

Make and join Blocks to desired size by the corner ps and by the 4 shells and 1 p on each side. To join ps, ch 2, sl st in corresponding p on 1st Block, ch 2, sl st back in last dc to complete p. To join shells, in place of center 3-ch, ch 2, sl st in corresponding shell on 1st Block, ch 2 back and complete shell with 3 dc.

EDGE—Join to 1st shell to right of one corner, * ch 8, tr in corner p, (ch 4, tr) 5 times in same p, ch 8, sc in next shell, ch 15, sc in next shell, ** ch 15, tr in next p, (ch 4, tr) 3 times in same p, (ch 15, sc in next shell) twice, ch 15, sc in joining of Blocks, (ch 15, sc in next shell) twice. Repeat from ** to last shell before next corner. Then repeat from * around cloth. **ROW 2**—* (5 sc, a p and 5 sc) in next 8-ch lp, (3 sc, a p, 3 sc) in each 4-ch sp, (5 sc, a p, 5 sc) in next lp, (5 sc, a p, sc, a p, 5 sc, a p and 5 sc) in each 15-ch lp. ** (3 sc, a p, 3 sc) in each 4-ch lp, (5 sc, a p, 5 sc, a p, 5 sc, a p and 5 sc) in each of next 6 lps. Repeat from ** up to 8-ch lp before shell at next

corner. Repeat from * around cloth. Fasten off. Stretch and pin tablecloth right-side-down in true shape on a padded board or table, or on curtain or quilting frames. Steam and press dry thru a cloth. If stretched on frames, lay over an ironing board and steam and press dry in sections until completed.

Afternoon Tea
Continued from page 15

30th Row. Ch 6, tr c in same space, * ch 4, 2 tr c with ch 2 between in next cluster st, repeat from * all around ending row with ch 4, join in 4th st of ch.

31st Row. Sl st into loop, ch 3, 2 d c in same space, * ch 5, skip 1 loop, 3 tr c with ch 2 between each tr c in next loop, ch 5, skip 1 loop, 3 d c in each of the next 3 loops, repeat from * all around ending row with ch 5, skip 1 loop, 3 tr c with ch 2 between each tr c in next loop, ch 5, skip 1 loop, 3 d c in each of the next 2 loops, join in 1st d c, turn.

32nd Row. Sl st in each of the next 3 d c, ch 3, turn, 1 d c in each of the next 2 d c, * ch 6, skip 1 loop, 2 tr c with ch 2 between in next loop, ch 3, 2 tr c with ch 2 between in next loop, ch 6, skip 3 d c, 1 d c in each of the next 3 d c, repeat from * all around ending row with ch 6, skip 1 loop, 2 tr c with ch 2 between in next loop, ch 3, 2 tr c with ch 2 between in next loop, ch 6, join in 3rd st of ch.

33rd Row. Sl st to next d c, ch 9, * skip 1 loop, 2 tr c with ch 2 between in next loop, ch 2, 3 tr c with ch 2 between each tr c in next loop, ch 2, 2 tr c with ch 2 between in next loop, ch 6, skip 1 d c, d c in next d c, ch 6, repeat from * all around ending row with skip 1 loop, 2 tr c with ch 2 between in next loop, ch 2, 3 tr c with ch 2 between each tr c in next loop, ch 2, 2 tr c with ch 2 between in next loop, ch 6, join in 3rd st of ch.

34th Row. Ch 7, sl st in 4th st from hook for picot. ** ch 2, skip 1 loop, tr c cluster st in next loop, (tr c cluster st: thread over needle twice, insert in space and work off 2 loops twice, * thread over needle twice, insert in same space and work off 2 loops twice, repeat from *, thread over and work off all loops at one time) ch 6, sl st in 4th st from hook for picot, * ch 4, sl st in same space for picot, repeat from *, ch 2, tr c cluster st in next loop, * ch 6, sl st in 4th st from hook for picot, ch 4, sl st in same space for picot, ch 4, sl st in same space for picot, ch 2, tr c cluster st in next loop, repeat from * 3 times, ch 2, d c in next d c, ch 4, sl st in top of d c for picot, repeat from ** all around.

Sunburst Splendor

MATERIALS:

CLARK'S O.N.T. or J. & P. COATS
BEST SIX CORD MERCERIZED CROCHET, size 30:

SMALL BALL:

CLARK'S O.N.T.—77 balls,
OR
J. & P. COATS —49 balls of White or Ecru, or 64 balls of any color.

BIG BALL:

J. & P. COATS—25 balls of White or Ecru, or 32 balls of any color.

Steel crochet hook No. 10 or 11.

GAUGE: Each motif measures about 4½ inches in diameter. For a tablecloth about 60 x 80 inches, make 13 x 17 motifs.

FIRST MOTIF . . . Ch 12. Join with sl st to form ring. **1st rnd:** Ch 1, 24 sc in ring. Join with sl st to 1st sc made. **2nd rnd:** Ch 7 (to count as d tr and ch-2), * d tr in next st, ch 2. Repeat from * around. Join last ch-2 to 5th st of ch-7. **3rd rnd:** Sl st in next sp, ch 4, tr in same sp, * ch 2, 2 tr in next sp. Repeat from * around. Join last ch-2 to 4th st of 1st ch. **4th rnd:** Sl st across to next sp, ch 1, sc in same sp, * ch 5, sc in next sp. Repeat from * around. Join last ch-5 to 1st sc. **5th rnd:** Sl st to center of 1st loop, ch 1, sc in same loop, * ch 5, sc in next loop. Repeat from * around. Join. **6th rnd:** Sl st in next loop, ch 3, 3 dc in same loop, * ch 3, sc in next loop, ch 3, 4 dc in next loop. Repeat from * around. Join last ch-3 to top st of 1st ch. **7th rnd:** Ch 3, dc in 3 dc, * ch 5, sc in next sc, ch 5, dc in 4 dc. Repeat from * around. Join. **8th rnd:** Ch 3, dc in 3 dc, * (ch 3, sc in next loop) twice; ch 3, dc in next 4 dc. Repeat from * around. Join. **9th rnd:** Ch 3, dc in 3 dc, 2 dc in next loop, * ch 4, sc in next loop, ch 4, 2 dc in next loop, dc in 4 dc, 2 dc in next loop. Repeat from * around, ending with 2 dc in last loop. Join. **10th rnd:** Ch 3, dc in 5 dc, 2 dc in next loop, * ch 3, 2 dc in next loop, dc in 8 dc, 2 dc in next loop. Repeat from * around. Join. **11th rnd:** Ch 7, * skip 2 dc, dc in next 5 dc, in next sp make 2 dc, ch 4 and 2 dc; dc in next 5 dc, ch 4. Repeat from * around. Join and fasten off.

SECOND MOTIF . . . Work as for 1st motif until 10th rnd is completed. **11th rnd:** Ch 7, skip 2 dc, dc in next 5 dc, 2 dc in next sp, ch 2, drop loop from hook, insert hook in corresponding ch-4 loop on 1st motif and pull dropped loop through, ch 2, 2 dc in same sp on 2nd motif, dc in next 5 dc, ch 2, join as before to next sp on 1st motif, ch 2, skip 2 dc on 2nd motif, dc in next 5 dc, 2 dc in next sp, ch 2, join to next ch-4 loop on 1st motif, ch 2, 2 dc in same sp on 2nd motif. Complete rnd same as 11th rnd of 1st motif (no more joinings). Fasten off.

Make necessary number of motifs, joining them as 2nd motif was joined to 1st motif, having two ch-4 sps and one ch-4 loop free between joinings.

FILL-IN-MOTIF . . . Ch 6. Join with sl st to form ring. **1st rnd:** Ch 1, 12 sc in ring. Join with sl st to 1st sc. **2nd rnd:** Ch 5 (to count as ch 2 and dc), * dc in next sc, ch 2. Repeat from * around, joining last ch-2 to 3rd st of ch-5 first made. **3rd rnd:** Sl st to next sp, ch 1, sc in same sp, * ch 4, sc in next sp.

Repeat from * around. Join. **4th rnd:** Sl st in next loop, ch 4, tr in same loop, * ch 5, 2 tr in next loop. Repeat from * around. Join. **5th rnd:** Sl st in next loop, ch 3, dc in same loop, * ch 2, join to free sp following joining of motifs, ch 2, 2 dc in same loop on Fill-in-motif, ch 5, 2 dc in next loop, ch 2, join to next loop on motif, ch 2, 2 dc in same loop on Fill-in-motif, ch 2, 2 dc in next loop, ch 2, join to next sp on motif, ch 2, 2 dc in same loop on Fill-in-motif, ch 5, 2 dc in next loop. Repeat from * around. Join and fasten off. Work Fill-in-motifs in this manner in all sps between joinings.

Detail of Pattern

Pineapple Luncheon Set

MATERIALS — DAISY Mercerized Crochet Cotton size 30:—4 skeins or balls White, Cream or Ecru (sufficient for Centerpiece, 4 Place Mats, 4 Bread and Butter Doilies and 4 Glass Doilies). Crochet hook size 12 or 13.

CENTERPIECE AND PLACE MATS —(14 inches)—**Pineapple**—Ch 10, sl st in 1st st. Ch 4, dc in ring, (ch 1, dc in ring) 13 times, ch 1, sl st in 3d st of 1st 4-ch. (2 sc in next sp) 15 times, sl st in 1st sc. (Ch 5, sc in next sc) 14 times. **ROW 4**—Ch 12, turn, sc in last lp, (ch 5, sc in next lp) repeated across to end 5-ch lp (1 less lp than last row). Repeate Row 4 twice. **ROW 7**—Ch 12, turn, sc in last lp, (ch 5, sc in next lp) 5 times, ch 5, sc in same center lp, (ch 5, sc in next lp) 5 times. * Repeat Row 4 twice. In next row, make an extra lp in center as in Row 7. Repeat from * once. Repeat Row 4 six times (one 5-ch lp in final row). Ch 12, turn, (sc, ch 12, sc) in single lp. Cut 6 inches long, thread to a needle and fasten off on back. Make 8 pineapples.

Center—Ch 8, sl st in 1st st. Ch 3, 17 dc in ring, sl st in 1st 3-ch. Work following rows in back lps only. **ROW 2**—Ch 3, dc in same st, (2 dc in next st) 17 times, sl st in 3-ch. **ROW 3**—Ch 3, dc in same st, (1 dc in next dc, 2 dc in next) repeated around and join. **ROW 4**—Ch 3, dc in same st, (dc in next 2 dc, 2 dc in next dc) repeated around and join. Repeat once. **ROW 6**—Ch 3, dc in same st, (dc in next 5 dc, 2 dc in next dc) repeated around and join. **ROW 7**—Ch 7, tr in next 2d dc, (ch 2, tr in next 2d dc) repeated around. Ch 2, sl st in 5th st of 1st 7-ch. **ROW 8**—Ch 3, (2 dc in next sp, dc in tr) repeated around. Sl st in 1st 3-ch. **ROW 9**—* Ch 5, 3 dtr in next 9th dc, holding back the last lp of each on hook, thread over and pull thru all 4 lps on hook at once (a Cluster made), (ch 5, a 3-dtr-Cluster in next dc) 3 times, ch 5, sc in next 9th dc. Repeat from * 7 times. **ROW 10**—Ch 7, a 2-dtr-Cluster in same st with last sc, * (ch 6, a 3-dtr-Cluster) 4 times in center sp of next shell, ch 6, a 3-dtr-Cluster in sc between shells. Repeat from * around. Join final 6-ch to 1st Cluster. **ROW 11**—Ch 10, * a 3-dtr-Cluster between next 2 Clusters, (ch 6, a Cluster) twice in next sp, ch 4, sl st in center sc on base of a pineapple, ch 4, (a Cluster, ch 6, a Cluster) back in same sp, a Cluster in next sp, ch 3, dtr in Cluster between shells, ch 3 and repeat from * around. Join final 3-ch to 7th st of 1st 10-ch. **ROW 12**—Ch 7, * a Cluster between next 2 Clusters, ch 6, a Cluster in next sp, (a 3 dc, ch 3, 3 dc shell in next 12-ch lp around pineapple) 9 times, ch 3, (a shell in next lp) 9 times, a Cluster between next 2 Clusters, ch 6, a Cluster in next sp, dtr in dtr between shells. Repeat from * around. Sl st in top of 1st 7-ch. Fasten off. **ROW 13**—Join to 3-ch sp at tip of a pineapple, ch 3, (2 dc, ch 3, 3 dc) in same sp, * (ch 1, a 3 dc, ch 3, 3 dc shell in next shell) 9 times, 3 sc in next 6-ch sp, sc in next 3 sts, 3 sc in next 6-ch, a shell in next shell, ch 1, 3 dc in next shell, ch 2, sl st back in 2d shell up side of previous pineapple, ch 2, 3 dc back in same shell, ch 1, 3 dc in next shell, ch 2, sl st back in next shell of 1st pineapple, ch 2, 3 dc back in same shell, ch 1, 3 dc in next shell, ch 8, turn, sl st in next shell on 1st pineapple, ch 1, turn, 8 sc and 1 sl st on 8-ch, ch 2, 3 dc in same shell, ch 1, 3 dc in next shell, ch 8, turn, a 3-dtr-Cluster in 4th sc, ch 6, a Cluster in next sc, ch 6, a Cluster in next shell. Ch 1, turn, (7 sc in next 6-ch) twice, 7 sc and 1 sl st in next lp, ch 2, 3 dc in same shell, ch 1, 3 dc in next shell, ch 8, turn, a 3-dtr-Cluster in center sc in next sp, ch 6, a Cluster in 3d sc in next sp, ch 6, a Cluster in next 2d sc, ch 6, a Cluster

in center sc in next sp, ch 6, sl st in next shell. Ch 1, turn, (4 sc, ch 5, sl st in last sc for a p, and 4 sc) in each of 5 sps, 1 sl st in same final sp, ch 2, 3 dc in same shell, (ch 1, a shell in next shell) 3 times, ch 1, a shell in next 3-ch sp. Repeat from * around. End with 1-ch, sl st in 1st 3-ch. Cut 6 inches long, thread to a needle and fasten off on back. Make 5.

BREAD AND BUTTER DOILY—**Pineapple**—Ch 10, sl st in 1st st. Ch 1, 15 sc in ring, sl st in 1st sc. (Ch 5, sc in next sc) 7 times. **ROW 3**—* Ch 12, turn, sc in last lp, (ch 5, sc in next lp) repeated across to end 5-ch. Repeat once. Make an added lp in center of next row. Repeat from * once. Repeat Row 3 twice (1 lp in final row). Ch 12, turn, (sc, ch 12, sc) in last lp. Fasten off on back. Make 6.

Center—Repeat Row 1 of "Center". **ROW 2**—Ch 7, tr in next dc, (ch 2, tr in next dc) 16 times, ch 2, sl st in 5th st of 1st 7-ch. **ROW 3**—Ch 3, (3 dc in next sp, dc in tr) repeated around, sl st in 3-ch. **ROW 4**—* Ch 7, (a 3-tr-Cluster, ch 6, a Cluster) in next 6th dc, ch 7, sc in next 6th dc. Repeat from * 5 times. **ROW 5**—Ch 9, * (a 3-dtr-Cluster, ch 6, a Cluster) between next 2 Clusters, ch 4, sl st in base of a pineapple, ch 4, (a Cluster, ch 6, a Cluster) in same sp with last Clusters, ch 2, dtr in sc between shells, ch 2 and repeat from * around. Join final 2-ch to 7th st of 1st 9-ch. **ROW 6**—Ch 1, * 2 sc in next 2-ch, sc in Cluster, 3 sc in next sp, (a 3 dc, ch 3 and 3 dc shell in next 12-ch lp on pineapple) 5 times, ch 3, (a shell in next lp) 5 times, 3 sc in next 6-ch sp, sc in Cluster, 2 sc in next 2-ch, sc in dtr. Repeat from * around. Fasten off. **ROW 7**—Join to 3-ch sp at tip of one pineapple, ch 3, (2 dc, ch 3, 3 dc) in same sp, * (ch 1, a shell in next shell) 5 times, dc in center sc between shells, 3 dc in next shell, ch 2, sl st back in last shell, ch 2, 3 dc back in same shell, ch 1, 3 dc in next shell, ch 8, turn, sl st in next shell on previous pineapple, ch 1, turn, (7 sc and 1 sl st) in 8-ch, ch 2, 3 dc in same shell, ch 1, 3 dc in next shell, ch 8, turn, a 3-dtr-Cluster in next 3d sc, ch 6, a Cluster in next 2d sc, ch 6, sl st in next shell. Ch 1, turn, (4 sc, a 5-ch p, 4 sc) in each of 3 sps, sl st in same final sp, ch 2, 3 dc in same shell, (ch 1, a shell in next shell) twice, ch 1, a shell in next 3-ch sp. Repeat from * around. Ch 1, sl st in 1st 3-ch. Fasten off on back. Make 4.

GLASS DOILY—Make 4 pineapples as in Bread and Butter Doily.

Center—Ch 8, sl st in 1st st. Ch 4, dc in ring, (ch 1, dc in ring) 10 times, ch 1, sl st in 3d st of 4-ch. **ROW 2**—

Continued on page 23

Summer Garden

Light-hearted butterflies circling around your luncheon table.

COATS & CLARK'S O.N.T. TATTING-CROCHET, Art. C.21, Size 70: 2 balls each of No. 8 Blue, No. 166 Lemon and Pink and 1 ball of No. 181 Shaded Lt. Yellows.

Milwards Steel Crochet Hook No. 13.

½ yard of yellow organdy, 36 inches wide.

Place Doily measures 15¼ inches in diameter; Bread and Butter Plate Doily measures 10 inches in diameter; Glass Doily measures 6½ inches in diameter.

PLACE DOILY—BUTTERFLY (Make 10)—Wing (Make 2) . . . Starting at lower edge with Lemon and Pink, ch 20. **1st row:** Tr in 8th ch from hook, tr in next ch, ch 2, skip 2 ch, dc in next 2 ch, ch 2, skip 2 ch, sc in next 4 ch; insert hook in next ch, draw loop through, drop Lemon and Pink, pick up Blue and draw a loop through, thus changing color. Ch 1, turn. **2nd row:** Sc in next 5 sts, (3 sc in next sp, sc in next 2 sts) twice; 15 sc in loop.

Now, working along opposite side of starting chain, (sc in next 2 ch, 3 sc in next sp) twice; sc in next 5 ch. Ch 1, turn. **3rd row:** Working in back loop only, sc in next 20 sc. Drop Blue. **4th row:** Pick up Lemon and Pink, draw loop through first sc, sc in same place, sc in next 4 sc, ch 3, skip 3 sc, dc in next 2 sc, ch 3, skip 3 sc, tr in next 2 sc, ch 3, skip 3 sc, tr tr in next sc, ch 2, skip next sc, tr tr in next sc. Pass ball of Lemon and Pink through loop on hook to secure st. Drop Lemon and Pink, pick up Blue. Turn. **5th row:** 15 sc over bar of tr tr, 4 sc in ch-2 sp, (sc in next 2 sts, 4 sc in next sp) 3 times; sc in next 5 sc. Ch 1, turn. **6th row:** Working in back loop only, sc in next 26 sc, insert hook in next sc, draw a loop through, drop Blue, pick up Lemon and Pink, draw a loop through. Ch 9, turn. **7th row:** Skip first sc, 2 d tr in next sc, ch 4, skip 2 sc, d tr in next 2 sc, ch 4, skip 4 sc, tr in next 2 sc, ch 4, skip 4 sc, dc in next 2 sc, ch 4, skip 4 sc, sc in next 5 sc; secure st by passing ball

through loop on hook. **8th row:** Pick up Blue, 20 sc in ch-9 loop, (sc in next 2 sts, 5 sc in next sp) 4 times; sc in next 5 sc. Ch 1, turn. **9th row:** Working in back loop only, sc in next 38 sc, drop Blue. **10th row:** Pick up Lemon and Pink, draw loop through first sc, sc in same place, sc in next 4 sc, ch 5, skip 5 sc, dc in next 2 sc, ch 5, skip 5 sc, tr in next 2 sc, (ch 5, skip 5 sc, d tr in next 2 sc) twice; ch 5, skip 2 sc, 2 d tr in next sc, ch 10, skip next sc, sl st in next sc. Break off. **11th row:** Pick up Blue, 21 sc in ch-10 loop, (sc in next 2 sts, 7 sc in next sp) 5 times; sc in next 5 sc. Break off.

BODY . . . With Lemon and Pink, ch 14. **1st row:** Sc in 2nd ch from hook, sc in next ch, half dc in next 2 ch, dc in next 4 ch, half dc in next 2 ch, sc in next 2 ch, sl st in last ch. Break off.

HEAD . . . With Blue, ch 8. Join with sl st to form ring. **1st rnd:** 20 sc in ring, sl st in side of first sc on Body,

Continued on page 29

21

Sheer Circles

MATERIALS... Choose one of the following threads in size 10, White or Ecru:

Clark's O.N.T. Mercerized Crochet, 27 balls.

J. & P. Coats Mercerized Crochet, 19 balls.

J. & P. Coats Big Ball Best Six Cord Mercerized Crochet, 11 balls.

Milward's steel crochet hook No. 9.

This material is sufficient for a set to serve four. Set consists of a centerpiece—18¾ inches in diameter; 4 plate doilies—12 inches; 4 bread and butter plate doilies—7½ inches; and 4 glass doilies—6 inches.

CENTERPIECE... Starting at center, ch 8, join with sl st to form ring. **1st rnd:** 20 s c in ring. Join with sl st to 1st s c made. **2nd rnd:** Ch 5 (to count as d c and ch-2), * skip 1 s c, d c in next s c, ch 2. Repeat from * around. Join with sl st to 3rd st of ch-5 first made (10 sps). **3rd rnd:** Sl st in next sp, ch 8 (to count as d c and ch-5), * d c in next sp, ch 5. Repeat from * around. Join with sl st to 3rd st of ch-8 first made. **4th rnd:** In each ch-5 sp around make: s c, half d c, 3 d c, half d c, s c. Join with sl st to 1st s c made (10 scallops). **5th rnd:** Ch 10 (to count as d c and ch-7); * d c between next 2 scallops, ch 7. Repeat from * around. Join with sl st to 3rd st of ch-10 first made. **6th rnd:** In each loop around make: s c, half d c, 7 d c, half d c, s c. Join. **7th rnd:** Ch 13 (to count as d c

Continued on next page

Lacy circles of frostlike tracings—a new doily luncheon set that lies sheer against dark, gleaming wood.

and ch-10), * d c between next 2 scallops, ch 10. Repeat from * around. Join. **8th rnd:** In each loop around make: s c, half d c, 10 d c, half d c, s c. Join. **9th rnd:** Ch 5 (to count as d c and ch-2), * skip 1st 3 sts of next scallop, s c in each of next 8 d c, ch 2, skip next 3 sts, d c between scallops, ch 2. Repeat from * around. Join to 3rd st of ch-5 first made. **10th rnd:** Ch 4 (to count as s c and ch-3), * skip next s c, s c in each of next 7 s c, ch 3, s c in next d c, ch 3. Repeat from * around. Join to 1st st of ch-4 first made. **11th rnd:** Ch 5 (to count as s c and ch-4), skip next s c, * s c in each of remaining 6 s c, ch 4, skip next sp, s c in next s c, ch 4, skip next sp and following s c. Repeat from * around. Join. **12th to 15th rnds incl:** Work as for 11th rnd, decreasing 1st s c of each s c-section and increasing 1 ch in each ch-section (2 s c and 8 ch on 15th rnd). Join. **16th rnd:** Ch 11, * skip next ch-8 and 1st s c of 2 s c-group, d c in next s c, ch 8, skip next ch-8, d c in next s c, ch 8. Repeat from * around. Join. **17th to 26th rnds incl:** Repeat 6th to 15th rnds incl. **27th and 28th rnds:** Repeat 16th and 6th rnds. **29th rnd:** Ch 12 (to count as d tr and ch-7), * d tr between next 2 scallops, ch 7. Repeat from * around. Join with sl st to 5th ch of ch-12 first made. **30th rnd:** same as 6th rnd. **31st and 32nd rnds:** Repeat 29th and 8th rnds. **33rd rnd:** Ch 15 (to count as d tr and ch-10), * d tr between next 2 scallops, ch 10. Repeat from * around, join. **34th rnd:** Same as 8th rnd. **35th to 41st rnds incl:** Repeat 9th to 15th rnds incl. **42nd and 43rd rnds:** Repeat 16th and 8th rnds. Do not break off, but make spokes as follows:

FIRST SPOKE... 1st row: Sl st across to 6th st of next scallop, s c in next st, ch 25, turn. **2nd row:** S c in 2nd ch from hook, s c in each ch across, sl st at base of foundation ch-25. Ch 1, turn. **3rd row:** S c in each s c across. Ch 1, turn. **4th row:** S c in each of 1st 4 s c, * ch 5, s c in each of next 4 s c. Repeat from * across, ending with s c in next st of scallop (five ch-5 loops). Ch 7, s c in 7th st of next scallop.

SECOND SPOKE...1st row: Ch 24, drop loop from hook, insert hook in 3rd (center) ch-5 loop, turn. **2nd row:** S c in each of 24 ch just made, sl st at base of ch-24, turn. **3rd and 4th rows:** Same as 3rd and

4th rows of first spoke. Continue making spokes, as for second spoke, all around to within last spoke.

LAST SPOKE...1st, 2nd and 3rd rows: Same as for previous spokes. **4th row:** S c in each of 1st 4 s c, ch 5, s c in each of next 4 s c, ch 5, s c in each of next 4 s c, ch 2, sl st in turning ch-2 at tip of 1st row of first spoke, ch 2, s c in each of next 4 s c on last spoke, and complete as for 4th row of previous spokes. Ch 8, join with sl st to base of first spoke made. Fasten and break off.

PLATE DOILY... Work as for centerpiece to 27th rnd incl. **28th rnd:** Repeat 8th rnd of centerpiece. Then work spokes all around as for centerpiece. Fasten and break off.

BREAD AND BUTTER PLATE DOILY... Work as for centerpiece to 16th rnd incl. **17th rnd:** Repeat 8th rnd of centerpiece. Then work spokes all around as for centerpiece.

GLASS DOILY... Ch 5, join with sl st to form ring. **1st rnd:** Ch 6 (to count as d c and ch-3), * d c in ring, ch 3. Repeat from * 3 more times. Join with sl st to 3rd st of ch-6 first made. **2nd rnd:** In each ch-3 sp around make: s c, half d c, 3 d c, half d c, s c. Join with sl st to s c first made (5 scallops made). **3rd rnd:** Ch 9 (to count as s c and ch-8), * s c between next 2 scallops, ch 8. Repeat from * around. Join to 1st st of ch-9 first made. **4th rnd:** In each loop around make: s c, half d c, 10 d c, half d c, s c. Join. **5th rnd:** Ch 5 (to count as d c and ch-2), * skip 1st 3 sts of next scallop, s c in each of next 8 d c, ch 2, d c between next 2 scallops, ch 2. Repeat from * around. Join with s c in 3rd st of ch-5 first made. **6th, 7th and 8th rnds:** Work over s c-groups as for previous doilies, but dec. 2 sts (1st and last s c) in each group, and inc. 2 ch in each section (2 s c and 8 ch on 8th rnd). Join. **9th rnd:** * Ch 10, skip next ch-8, s c between 2 s c of next group, ch 10, skip next ch-8, s c in next s c. Repeat from * around, join. **10th rnd:** In each loop around make: s c, half d c, 10 d c, half d c, s c. Join. Then work spokes as for centerpiece, but make ch-10 (instead of ch-7) between spokes, and join spokes at 4th loop made on each spoke (instead of center loop). Fasten and break off.

Pineapple Luncheon Set
Continued from page 20

(2 sc in next 1-ch sp) 12 times. Sl st in 1st sc. **ROW 3**— * Ch 6, a 3-tr-Cluster in next 3d sc, ch 3, sl st in center sc at base of one pineapple, ch 3, a Cluster in same sc on Center, ch 6, sc in next 3d sc. Repeat from * 3 times. Fasten off on back. **ROW 4**—Join to 5th 12-ch lp up right side of one pineapple, ch 3, (2 dc, ch 3, 3 dc) in * ch 3, (a 3 dc, ch 3, 3 dc shell in next lp) 5 times, (a 3-dtr-Cluster in next 6-ch lp) twice, 3 dc in 1st 12-ch lp on next pineapple, ch 2, sl st back in last shell, ch 2, 3 dc back in same lp, (a shell in next lp) 4 times. Repeat from * around. Sl st to center of shell. **ROW 5**—Ch 3, (2 dc,

ch 3, 3 dc) in same shell, * ch 1, a shell in next 3-ch sp, (ch 1, a shell in next shell) 4 times, tr in joining of next 2 shells, 3 dc in next shell, ch 7, turn, sl st in next shell, ch 1, turn, 7 sc and 1 sl st in 7-ch, ch 2, 3 dc in same shell, ch 1, 3 dc in next shell, ch 8, turn, a 3-dtr-Cluster in 3d sc on center lp, ch 6, a Cluster in next 2d sc, ch 6, sl st in next shell. Ch 1, turn, (4 sc, a 5-dc p and 4 sc) in each of 3 sps, sl st in same last sp, ch 2, 3 dc in same shell, (ch 1, a shell in next shell) twice. Repeat from * around and join. Fasten off on back. Make 4.

Pin doilies right-side-down in true shape, stretching several inches to open out pattern. Steam and press dry thru a cloth.

23

Daffodil
Luncheon Set

Materials Required—

AMERICAN THREAD COMPANY
"PURITAN" MERCERIZED CROCHET AND
KNITTING COTTON. ARTICLE 40

9—200 yd. Balls Yellow or any Color desired—will make 4 doilies.

Steel Crochet Hook #7.

Each doily measures about 19 inches in diameter.

Ch 6, join to form a ring, ch 1 and work 8 s c in ring, do not join this or the following rows, place a marker at beginning of each row.

2nd Row—2 s c in each s c.

3rd Row—Working in s c, increase in every other st.

4th Row—Increase in every 3rd s c.

5th Row—Increase in every 4th s c.

6th Row—Increase in every 5th s c, then work 1 row even.

8th Row—Increase in every 6th s c.

9th Row—Increase in every 7th s c, then work 1 row even.

11th Row—Increase in every 8th s c.

12th Row—Increase in every 9th s c, then work 1 row even.

14th Row—Increase in every 10th s c.

15th Row—Increase in every 11th s c.

16th Row—Increase in every 12th s c. Repeat the 11th, 12th, 13th and 14th rows.

21st & 22nd Rows—Work even.

23rd Row—Increase in every 11th s c, then work 5 rows even.

29th Row—Increase in every 6th s c, then work 4 rows even.

34th Row—Increase in every 7th s c, then work 1 row even.

36th Row—Increase in every 8th s c, then work 4 rows even.

41st Row—Increase in every 9th s c, then work 3 rows even.

45th Row—Increase in every 10th s c, then work 4 rows even.

50th Row—Increase in every 11th s c, then work 4 rows even (312 s c), sl st in next 2 s c to even row.

55th Row—* Ch 6, skip 3 s c, s c in next s c, repeat from * all around ending row with ch 3, d c in same st with the 1st ch 6, this brings thread in position for next row (78 loops).

56th Row—* Ch 7, s c in next loop, repeat from * all around ending row with ch 3, tr c in d c.

57th Row—Same as last row ending row with ch 3, tr c in tr c.

58th Row—Same as last row but having 8 chs in each loop and ending row with ch 4, tr c in tr c.

59th Row—Ch 4, s c in same loop ** ch 4, 2 cluster sts with ch 5 between in next loop (cluster st: thread over needle, insert in loop, pull through and work off 2 loops, * thread over needle, insert in same space, pull through and work off 2 loops, repeat from *, thread over and work off all loops at one time), ch 4, s c in next loop, ch 4, s c in same loop (picot loop) repeat from ** all around ending row with ch 4, 2 cluster sts with ch 5 between in next loop, ch 4, join in base of 1st picot loop.

60th Row—Sl st into the picot loop, * ch 7, s c in ch 5 loop between next 2 cluster sts, ch 4, s c in same space (picot loop), ch 7, s c in next picot loop, repeat from * all around ending row with ch 4, tr c in sl st.

61st Row—Ch 8, d c in same loop, * ch 5, sl st in 4th st from hook for picot, ch 1, 1 d c, ch 5, 1 d c (shell) in next ch 7 loop, repeat from * all around ending row with ch 5, sl st in 4th st from hook for picot, ch 1, join in 3rd st of ch.

62nd Row—Sl st into shell, * ch 4, s c in same space, ch 8, skip the picot, s c in center of next shell, repeat from * all around ending row with ch 4, s c in same space, ch 4, tr c in sl st.

63rd Row—Same as 61st row working a shell in each 8 ch loop.

64th Row—Sl st into shell and work 2 cluster sts with ch 5 between in same space, * ch 6, s c in next shell, ch 4, s c in same space, ch 6, 2 cluster sts with ch 5 between in next shell, repeat from * all around ending row with ch 6, s c, ch 4, s c in next loop, ch 6, join in top of 1st cluster st.

65th Row—Sl st into loop, * ch 4, s c in same space, ch 9, s c in next picot loop, ch 9, 1 s c, ch 4, 1 s c between next 2 cluster sts, repeat from * all around in same manner ending row with ch 4, d tr c in sl st.

66th Row—* Ch 10, s c in next ch 9 loop, repeat from * all around ending row with ch 5, tr tr c (4 times over needle) in d tr c.

67th Row—* Ch 10, s c in next loop, repeat from * all around ending row same as last row.

68th Row—Ch 1, s c in same space, * ch 6, 2 cluster sts with ch 6 between in next loop, ch 6, s c in next loop, repeat from * all around, join in 1st s c.

69th Row—Ch 1, s c in same s c, ** ch 6, cluster st between next 2 cluster sts, * ch 5, sl st in 4th st from hook for picot, ch 1, cluster st in same space, repeat from * twice, ch 6, s c in next s c, repeat from ** all around, break thread.

Enchantress

MATERIALS:

CLARK'S O.N.T. or J. & P. COATS BIG BALL BEST SIX CORD MERCERIZED CROCHET, size 30:

CLARK'S O.N.T.—26 balls of White or Ecru.

J. & P. COATS—26 balls of White or Ecru, or 35 balls of any color.

MILWARD'S Steel Crochet Hook No. 10.

GAUGE . . . Each motif measures 5 inches from point to opposite point. Completed tablecloth measures about 70 x 90 inches.

FIRST MOTIF . . . Starting at center, ch 10, join with sl st. **1st rnd:** Ch 1, 16 s c in ring; join. **2nd rnd:** Ch 5 (to count as d tr); make 4 d tr in same place as sl st, holding back on hook the last loop of each d tr; thread over and draw through all loops on hook (a cluster made). * Ch 10, skip 1 s c, make 5 d tr in next s c, holding back on hook the last loop of each d tr; thread over and draw through all loops on hook (another cluster). Repeat from * around. Join last ch-10 to tip of 1st cluster made. **3rd rnd:** In each ch-10 loop around make 5 s c, ch 5 and 5 s c. **4th rnd:** Sl st in each of next 5 s c in and in next ch-5 loop, s c in loop, ch 6 (to count as d tr and ch-1). In loop make 7 d tr separated by ch-1. In each loop around make 8 d tr separated by ch-1; join. **5th rnd:** * S c in next sp; (ch 5, s c in next sp) 6 times; ch 1, skip next 2 d tr. Repeat from * around; join.

6th rnd: Sl st in 1st 2 sts of next loop, s c in loop. * (Ch 5, s c in next loop) 5 times; ch 3, s c in next loop. Repeat from * around; join. **7th rnd:** Sl st in 1st 2 sts of next loop, s c in loop; * (ch 5, s c in next loop) 4 times; ch 5, skip next ch-3, s c in next loop. Repeat from * around; join. **8th rnd:** Sl st in 1st 2 sts of next loop, s c in loop, * ch 5, s c in next loop. Repeat from * around; join. **9th rnd:** Sl st in 1st 2 sts of next loop, s c in loop; * (ch 5, s c in next loop) twice, ch 6, s c in next loop, s c in next s c, s c in next loop, ch 6, s c in next loop. Repeat from * around; join. **10th rnd:** Sl st to center of next loop, s c in loop; * ch 5, s c in next loop, ch 8, s c in next loop, s c in next 3 s c and in following loop; ch 8, s c in next loop. Repeat from * around; join.

11th rnd: S c in next loop, ch 5 (to count as d tr); make 4 d tr in same loop, holding back on hook the last loop of each d tr, and complete cluster as before. Ch 10, in same loop make two 5-d tr clusters separated by ch-10. * Ch 5, s c in next loop, s c in next 5 s c and in following loop, ch 5; in next loop make 3 clusters separated by

ch-10. Repeat from * around; join. **12th rnd:** * In each of next two ch-10 loops make (3 s c, ch 3) 3 times and 3 s c. In next ch-5 loop make 3 s c, ch 3 and 3 s c; s c in each of next 7 s c. In next ch-5 loop make 3 s c, ch 3 and 3 s c. Repeat from * around. Join and fasten off. This completes one motif.

SECOND MOTIF . . . Work 1st 11 rnds as for first motif. **12th rnd:** In next ch-10 loop make (3 s c, ch 3) 3 times and 3 s c. In next loop make 3 s c, ch 3 and 3 s c. Ch 1, s c in corresponding ch-3 picot on first motif, ch 1, 3 s c back in same loop of second motif. Ch 3, 3 s c in same loop. In next ch-5 loop make 3 s c, ch 3 and 3 s c; s c in next 7 s c. In next ch-5 loop make 3 s c, ch 3 and 3 s c. In next ch-10 loop make 3 s c, ch 3 and 3 s c. Ch 1, s c in corresponding picot on first motif, ch 1, 3 s c back in same loop of second motif; complete rnd as for first motif (no more joinings).

Make 13 x 17 motifs, joining 2 picots of each motif to 2 picots of adjacent motifs as second motif was joined to first (see illustration).

FILL-IN LACE . . . Starting at center, ch 10, join. **1st rnd:** 16 s c in ring; join. **2nd rnd:** Ch 5 (to count as d tr) and make a cluster as before in same place as sl st was made; ch 7, sl st in center picot on a free ch-10 loop of a motif. * Ch 7, skip 1 s c on ring, make a 5-d tr cluster in next s c, ch 7, sl st in center picot on next ch-10 loop on motif. Repeat from * around. Join and fasten off. Fill in all spaces in this manner. Block cloth to measurements given.

Sheer Witchery

MATERIALS—DAISY Mercerized Crochet Cotton, size 30, in White, Cream or Ecru: 3-skeins are sufficient for Centerpiece 18″ in diameter, 4-Place Mats 14″ in diameter, 4-Bread and Butter Doilies 7½″ in diameter, and 4-Glass Doilies 6″ in diameter. Crochet hook size 10.

CENTERPIECE—Ch 7, sl st in 1st st. Ch 3, 17 dc in ring, sl st in 3-ch. **ROW 2**—Ch 3, dc in same st, (2 dc in next dc) 17 times and join. **ROW 3**—Ch 3, (2 dc in next dc) twice, 1 dc in next, ch 11, remove hook, insert it back in 3d ch st from last dc, catch lp and pull thru, (ch 4, 2 sc in ring) 7 times, * ch 2, sl st under 2-ch stem, (2 dc in next dc) twice, 1 dc in next, ch 11 and form a ring as before, ch 4, 2 sc in ring, ch 2, sl st back in 2d p on previous flower, ch 2, 2 sc back in ring, (ch 4, 2 sc in ring) 5 times. Repeat from * thru 11 flowers. (2 dc in next dc) twice, sl st in 1st 3-ch and make 12th flower. Fasten off. Tack 1st and last flowers together. **ROW 4**—Join to center p on one flower, (ch 10, sc in next flower repeated around. **ROW 5**—Ch 3, (11 dc in next sp, 1 dc in sc) repeated around and join. **ROW 6**—Ch 3, (dc in 6 dc and make a flower as in Row 3) repeated thru 23 flowers. 5 dc, sl st in 1st 3-ch and make 24th flower. Fasten off. Tack 1st and last flowers together. **ROW 7**—Like Row 4 but with 9-ch lps. **ROW 8**—Ch 3, * (10 dc in next sp, 1 dc in sc) twice, 9 dc in next sp, 1 dc in sc. Repeat from * around and join. **ROW 9**—Ch 3, (dc in 8 dc and make a flower as in Row 3) repeated thru 31 flowers, 7 dc, sl st in 1st 3-ch and make 32d flower. Fasten off. Tack 1st and last flowers together. **ROW 10**—Repeat Row 4. **ROW 11**—Ch 3, (10 dc in next sp, 1 dc in sc) repeated around and join. **ROW 12**—Ch 3, 1 dc in each dc and join. **ROW 13**—Ch 1, sc in next 3 dc, * (ch 5, sc in 4th ch st from hook for a p, ch 2, 1 tr) 4 times in next 8th dc, ch 5, p, ch 2, sk 7 dc, sc in next 7 dc. Repeat from * 15 times. ending

Continued on next page

with 3 sc, sl st in 1st 1-ch. **ROW 14**—Ch 9 for a dtr, turn, * (ch 5, p, ch 2, dtr) 6 times in center p of next shell, ch 5, p, ch 2, dtr in center sc between shells. Repeat from * around, joining to 9th ch st with sl st. **ROW 15**—Ch 9 for a dtr, turn, * ch 6, p, ch 2, dtr in center p of next shell, (ch 5, p, ch 2, dtr) 7 times in same p, ch 5, p, ch 3, dtr between shells. Repeat from * around and join to 9th ch st. **ROW 16**—Ch 11 for a tr tr, turn, * ch 6, p, ch 3, tr tr in next shell, (ch 5, p, ch 2, tr tr) 7 times in same place, ch 6, p, ch 3, tr tr between shells. Repeat from * around and join to 11th ch st. **ROW 17**—Ch 11 for a tr tr, turn, * ch 8, p, ch 4, tr tr in next shell, (ch 5, p, ch 2, tr tr) 7 times in same place, ch 7, p, ch 5, tr tr between shells. Repeat from * around and join to 11th ch st. For a small table, fasten off here. For a large table, continue with **ROW 18** —Ch 13 for a long tr, turn, * ch 9, p, ch 5, ** a long tr (thread over 5 times and work off in twos) in next shell, (ch 5, p, ch 2, a long tr) 7 times in same place, ** ch 8, p, ch 6, a long tr between shells. Repeat from * around and join to 13th ch st. **ROW 19**—Ch 15 for an extra long tr, turn, * ch 11, p, ch 7 and repeat from ** to ** in last row. Ch 10, p, ch 8, an extra long tr (thread over 6 times) be-

tween shells. Repeat from * around and join to 15th ch st. Fasten off. **PLACE MAT**—Repeat thru Row 17. For a small table, repeat thru Row 16, except do not turn at start of Row 16.

BREAD AND BUTTER PLATE DOILY—Repeat thru Row 5. Repeat Row 12. **ROW 7**—Ch 1, sc in next 2 dc, * (ch 5, p, ch 2, tr) 4 times in next 7th dc, ch 5, p, ch 2, sk 6 dc, sc in next 5 dc. Repeat from * 7 times, ending with 2 sc, sl st in 1st 1-ch. **ROW 8**—Ch 9 for a dtr, turn, * (ch 5, p, ch 2, tr tr) 8 times in center p of next shell, ch 5, p, ch 2, dtr in center sc between shells. Repeat from * around and join to 10th ch st. ** Repeat Row 17. Fasten off.

GLASS DOILY—Repeat Bread and Butter Plate Doily to ** except do not turn at start of Row 8. Stretch and pin doilies right-side-down in true circles on a padded board. Pat with a cloth pad dipped in thin, hot starch. Press partly dry thru a cloth. Remove pins, loosen doilies from board, pin down lightly on a fresh cloth on board and let remain until dry.

Snow Crystal
Continued from page 9

This material is sufficient for 4 place mats, each about 11½ x 21½ inches, and a center mat about 11½ x 34 inches. This set is made in individual wheels and then sewed together.
Place Mat. Wheel. Beginning at center, ch 12, join with sl st to form ring. **1st row:** Ch 21 (to measure 1¾ inches). S c in 2nd ch from hook and in each ch across (20 s c). Make 1 s c in ring. Ch 1, turn.
2nd row: Picking up only the back loop of each s c, skip 1st s c, s c in each of next 20 s c. Ch 1, turn.
3rd row: Picking up only the back loop of each s c, s c in each of next 4 s c, * ch 5, s c in each of next 4 s c, repeat from * across, ending with 4 s c (4 p's made). Make 1 s c in ring. This completes the first spoke. Do not break off but continue for the second spoke. **Second Spoke: 1st row:** Ch 20, drop loop from hook, insert hook in 2nd p from ring and draw dropped loop through. S c in each ch st of ch-20 (20 s c). Make 1 s c in ring. Ch 1, turn. Repeat the 2nd and 3rd rows of first spoke once. Then make 4 more spokes same as second spoke (6 in all), but while making the 3rd p of the 6th spoke, attach to 1st spoke by making ch 2, sl st in end s c of 1st spoke, ch 2, and continue back on 6th spoke as usual. Fasten and break off. This completes one wheel. Make 33 more wheels.
Joining: Place wheels in position (as in illustration)—a row of 8 wheels for the center row, a row of 7 wheels along each side of center row, and a row

of 6 wheels along each side of these two rows. Pin ends of spokes together (as marked on illustration of stitch detail) in corresponding position and then sew them together on wrong side with over and over stitches. Make 3 more place mats.
Center Mat. Make 59 wheels and join as in place mat, having a row of 13 wheels for the center row, a row of 12 wheels along each side of center row, and a row of 11 wheels along each side of these two rows.

Summer Garden
Continued from page 21

sc in each st across Body, 3 sc in sl st at other end of Body; working across opposite side, sc in each ch across, sl st in first sc on Head. Break off.

ANTENNAE . . . With Lemon and Pink, ch 25. Break off. Attach Blue to first ch, ch 3, dc in same ch, ch 3, sl st in same ch, sl st in each ch across to center, sl st in center of Head, sl st in each remaining chain across, ch 3, dc in last ch, ch 3, sl st in same ch. Break off.

Sew Wings and Body together. Sew Butterflies together, joining center of loops on last row of each wing. Place Butterflies on organdy and trace around inside edges. Cut out material in back of Butterflies, leaving ⅛ inch for hem. Sew hem and Butterflies neatly in place.

EDGING . . . Attach Shaded Lt. Yellows to right side of Antennae on any Butterfly, sc in same place, * ch 15, sc in end of left side of same Antenna, ch 10, skip 2 sps on wing, in center sc of next sp make tr, ch 10 and tr; ch 10, skip next sp, sc in center sc of next sp,

ch 10, skip 5 sc on next sp, tr in next sc, tr in corresponding sc of next wing, ch 10, sc in center sc of next sp, ch 10, skip next sp, in center sc of next sp make tr, ch 10 and tr; ch 10, sc in end of next Antenna. Repeat from * around. Join and break off.

BREAD AND BUTTER PLATE DOILY . . . Make 6 Butterflies. Sew together as before and complete as for Place Doily.

GLASS DOILY . . . Make 4 Butterflies and complete as for Place Doily.
Starch lightly and press.

Summer Snowflake

Shown on page 12

GAUGE: Each motif measures 4½ inches from loop to loop across center. For a tablecloth 72 x 90 inches, make 16 x 20 motifs.

FIRST MOTIF . . . Starting at center, ch 10. Join with sl st. **1st rnd:** Ch 3, 23 dc in ring, sl st in top of ch-3. **2nd rnd:** Ch 3, dc in next 2 dc, * ch 5, dc in next 3 dc. Repeat from * around, ending with ch 5, sl st in top of ch-3. **3rd rnd:** Ch 3, dc in next 2 dc, * ch 3, sc in next sp, ch 3, dc in next 3 dc. Repeat from * around, ending with ch 3, join. **4th rnd:** Ch 3, dc in next 2 dc, * ch 5, then holding back on hook the last loop of each dc, work dc in next 2 sps, thread over and draw through all loops on hook, ch 5, dc in next 3 dc. Repeat from * around, ending with ch 5, join. **5th rnd:** Ch 3, dc in next 2 dc, 3 dc in next sp, * ch 9, 3 dc in next sp, dc in next 3 dc, 3 dc in next sp. Repeat from * around, ending with 3 dc in last sp, sl st in top of ch-3. **6th rnd:** Ch 3, dc in next 3 dc, * ch 11, skip next sp and 2 dc of next dc-group, dc in next

5 dc. Repeat from * around, ending with ch 11, skip 2 dc in last dc. Join. **7th rnd:** Ch 3, then holding back on hook the last loop of each dc, work dc in next 2 dc, thread over and draw through all loops on hook (cluster made), * ch 9, sc in ch-9 loop 2 rnds below (working over both ch bars), ch 9, skip 1 dc, then holding back on hook the last loop of each dc work dc in next 3 dc, thread over and draw through all loops on hook. Repeat from * around. Join last ch-9 with sl st to tip of 1st cluster. **8th rnd:** Sl st in next, 4 ch, sc in loop, * ch 13, sc in next loop. Repeat from * around, ending with sl st in 1st sc made. **9th rnd:** Sl st in next 6 ch, sc in loop, * ch 15, sc in next loop. Repeat from * around, ending as before. Fasten off.

SECOND MOTIF . . . Work as for 1st motif to 8th rnd incl. **9th rnd:** Sl st in next 6 ch, sc in loop, * ch 7, sc in corresponding loop of 1st motif, ch 7, sc in next loop on motif in work. Repeat from * once more and complete rnd as for 1st motif (no more joinings).

Make necessary number of motifs, joining them as 2nd motif was joined to 1st, leaving two free loops on each motif between joinings.

FILL-IN-MOTIF . . . Ch 10, join. **1st rnd:** Ch 3, 23 dc in ring. Join. **2nd rnd:** Ch 4, then holding back on hook the last loop of each tr work 2 tr in same place as sl st, thread over and draw through all loops on hook (cluster made), ch 4, sc in a free loop of large motif, * ch 4, skip 2 dc on Fill-in-motif, make a 3-tr cluster in next dc, ch 4, sc in next free loop of large motif. Repeat from * around, ending with ch 4, sl st in tip of 1st cluster made. Fasten off. Fill in all sps between joinings in this manner.

EDGING . . . Attach thread to joining between any 2 large motifs, * 7 sc in 1st loop of next motif; in each free ch-15 loop of same motif make sc, h dc, 5 dc, 4 tr, 5 dc, h dc and sc; then work 7 sc in last loop (preceding joining). Repeat from * around. Join, fasten off.

Ardmore

Shown on page 13

MATERIALS:

CLARK'S O.N.T. or J. & P. COATS BEST SIX CORD MERCERIZED CROCHET
SIZE 30

SMALL BALL:
CLARK'S O.N.T.—*112 balls of White or Ecru, or 168 balls of any color,*

OR

J. & P. COATS—*84 balls of White or Ecru, or 112 balls of any color.*

BIG BALL:
CLARK'S O.N.T.—*42 balls of White or Ecru,*

OR

J. & P. COATS—*42 balls of White or Ecru, or 55 balls of any color.*

Milward's Steel Crochet Hook *No. 10 or 11.*

GAUGE: Each motif measures 3½ inches from point to opposite point across center before blocking. For a tablecloth 72 x 108 inches, make 20 x 30 motifs.

FIRST MOTIF . . . Starting at center, ch 8. Join with sl st. **1st rnd:** Ch 3, 23 dc in ring. Join with sl st to 3rd st of ch-3 first made. **2nd rnd:** Ch 3, dc in next 2 dc, * ch 3, dc in next 3 dc. Repeat from * around, ending with ch 3, sl st in 3rd st of ch-3 first made. **3rd rnd:** Ch 3, dc in next 2 dc, * ch 5, dc in next 3 dc. Repeat from * around, ending with ch-5; join rnd as before. **4th rnd:** Ch 3, dc in next 2 dc, * ch 7, dc in next 3 dc. Repeat from * around, ending with ch 7; join. **5th rnd:** Ch 3, dc in next 2 dc, * ch 5, sc in next sp, ch 5, dc in next 3 dc. Repeat from * around, ending with ch-5; join. **6th rnd:** Ch 3, dc in next 2 dc holding back on hook the last loop of each dc, thread over and draw through all loops on hook (cluster made); * (ch 5, sc in next loop) twice, ch 5, dc in next 3 dc holding back on hook the last loop of each dc and complete

cluster as before. Repeat from * around, ending with ch-5, sl st in tip of 1st cluster made. **7th rnd:** Sl st in next 2-ch, sc in loop, * (ch 5, sc in next loop) twice; ch 9, sc in next loop. Repeat from * around, ending with ch-9, sl st in first sc made. **8th rnd:** Sl st in next 2 ch, sc in loop, * ch 5, sc in next loop, ch 1, dc in next loop (ch 1, dc in same loop) 7 times; ch 1, sc in next loop. Repeat from * around, ending with ch-1, sl st in 1st sc made. **9th rnd:** 3 sc in ch-5 loop, sc in next ch-1 sp, (ch 3, sc in next ch-1 sp) 8 times. Repeat from beginning of rnd, ending with sl st in 1st sc made. Fasten off.

SECOND MOTIF . . . Work as for 1st motif to 8th rnd incl. **9th rnd:** 3 sc in ch-5 loop, sc in next ch-1 sp, (ch 3, sc in next ch-1 sp) 3 times; ch 1, sl st in corresponding loop on 1st motif (thus joining motifs), ch 1, sc in next ch-1 sp, join next loop to corresponding loop on 1st motif as before and continue as for 1st motif (no more joinings). Make 16 x 22 motifs and join them as 2nd motif was joined to 1st (one point free between joinings).

FILL-IN-MOTIF . . . Starting at center, ch 8. Join with sl st. **1st rnd:** Ch 3, 23 dc in ring. Join with sl st to 3rd st of ch-3 first made. **2nd rnd:** Sc in same place as sl st, ch 16, sl st in joining of motifs, h dc in each ch across, skip 1 dc, sc in next dc, * ch 6, skip 2 loops on free point of large motif; sl st in next loop, h dc in each st across, skip 1 dc, sc in next dc. Repeat from * once more. Now repeat from beginning of rnd, ending with sl st in sc at base of ch-16 first made. Fasten off. Work fill-in-motifs in this manner in all sps between joinings.

EDGINGS

Edgings for Your Finest Things

WE SUGGEST ROYAL SOCIETY CORDICHET, SIZES 30-50

No. 3-14 . . . EDGING . . . Starting at narrow end, ch 6. **1st row:** In 6th ch from hook make dc, ch 2 and dc. Ch 5, turn. **2nd row:** In ch-2 sp make dc, ch 2 and dc. Ch 5, turn. Repeat 2nd row for length desired, having a multiple of 4 plus 3 dc groups. Ch 2, do not turn but work scallops along long edge of piece as follows: **1st row:** * In next ch-5 loop make 4 dc, ch 3 and 4 dc. Repeat from * across. Ch 3, turn. **2nd row:** * In next ch-3 sp make (tr, ch 5) 3 times and tr; sc in next ch-3 sp. Repeat from * across, ending with dc in turning ch-2. Ch 1, turn. **3rd row:** * In next loop make 3 sc, ch 3 and 3 sc; in center loop make (2 sc, ch 3) 3 times and 2 sc; in next loop make 3 sc, ch 3 and 3 sc, sc in next sc. Repeat from * across, ending with sc in turning ch. Fasten off.

INSERTION . . . Ch 6 and work 1st and 2nd rows same as Edging. Ch 2, do not turn but work along long edge as follows: **1st row:** * In next ch-5 loop make 4 dc, ch 3 and 4 dc. Repeat from * across. Turn. **2nd row:** Sl st in 4 dc, sl st in sp, ch 1, sc in same sp, * ch 5, sc in next sp. Repeat from * across. Fasten off. With right side facing, attach thread in 1st ch-5 loop on opposite edge and work to correspond. Fasten off.

No. 3-15 . . . Ch 11. **1st row:** Dc in 8th ch from hook, dc in next 3 ch. Ch 7, turn. **2nd to 8th rows incl:** Dc in 4 dc. Ch 7, turn. At end of 8th row, ch 3, sc in next loop on this edge, dc in next loop. Ch 3, turn. **9th row:** Dc in 4 dc, ch 7, turn. **10th row:** Dc in 4 dc, ch 2, sc in sc on opposite loop, ch 2, turn. **11th row:** Dc in 4 dc, ch 7, turn. **12th row:** Dc in 4 dc, ch 2, dc in dc on opposite loop, ch 2, turn. **13th and 14th rows:** Dc in 4 dc. Ch 7, turn. At end of 14th row, ch 2, 2 tr in corresponding loop on opposite side. Ch 3, turn. **15th and 16th rows:** Repeat 13th and 14th rows. **17th row:** Dc in 4 dc. Ch 16, turn. **18th row:** Dc in 8th ch from hook, dc in next 3 ch. Ch 3, sc in next free loop on opposite edge. Ch 3, turn. **19th row:** Dc in 4 dc. Ch 7, turn. **20th row:** Dc in 4 dc, ch 3, dc in next free loop on opposite edge. Ch 3, turn. **21st row:** Dc in 4 dc. Ch 7, turn. **22nd row:** Dc in 4 dc, ch 3, tr in next free loop on opposite edge. Ch 3, turn. Repeat the last 17 rows (6th to 22nd rows inclusive) for length desired. Fasten off.

EDGING . . . Attach thread in 4th loop on 1st scallop, ch 8, sc in 4th ch from hook (p made), * (dc in same loop, p) twice; dc in same loop, dc in next loop, (p, dc in same loop) 3 times; ch 4, tr over joining tr, ch 4, dc in next free loop, p. Repeat from * across.

No. 3-16 . . . Starting at narrow end, ch 18. **1st row:** Dc in 8th ch from hook and in next 6 ch, ch 5, sk 3 ch, dc in next ch. Ch 10, turn. **2nd row:** 3 dc in sp, dc in next dc, ch 2, sk 2 dc, dc in next 4 dc. Ch 7, turn. **3rd row:** Dc in 4 dc, 2 dc in sp, dc in next dc, ch 5, sk 2 dc, dc in next dc. Ch 10, turn. Repeat the 2nd and 3rd rows alternately for length desired, ending with 2nd row, making sure that there are an odd number of ch-10 turning loops. Do not fasten off, but ch 7 to turn and work along lower edge as follows: **Next row:** Dc in 4 dc, 2 dc in sp, dc in next dc, ch 10, * 3 dc in next ch-10 loop, ch 3, 3 dc in same loop. Repeat from * across. Turn. **Following row:** Sl st to center of ch-3 sp, sc in same sp, * ch 3, tr in next ch-3 sp, (ch 5, dc in tr just made, tr in same place as last tr) 3 times; ch 3, sc in next ch-3 sp. Repeat from * across, ending with sc in last ch-3 sp. Fasten off.

HEADING . . . Attach thread to 1st ch-7 loop at top of edging, sc in same place, * ch 5, sc in next ch-7 loop. Repeat from * across. Fasten off.

3-14

3-15

3-16

33

8850

8883

Delicate Touches

TO ADD GLAMOUR
TO FINE FINGERTIP
OR GUEST TOWELS,
AND HANKIES

No. 8850 . . . Ch 21. **1st row:** Sc in 2nd ch from hook, h dc in next ch, dc in next ch, tr in next ch, (ch 2, skip 2 ch, tr in each of next 2 ch) 4 times. Ch 4, turn. **2nd row:** Tr in next tr, ch 5, sc in each of next 2 tr, ch 5, tr in each of next 2 tr, ch 5, sc in each of next 2 tr. Ch 7, turn. **3rd row:** Sc in 2nd ch from hook, h dc in next ch, dc in next ch, tr in next ch, ch 2, tr in next 2 sc, ch 2, sc in next 2 tr, ch 2, tr in next 2 sc, ch 2, sc in next tr, sc in top st of turning ch. Ch 4, turn. **4th row:** Tr in next sc, ch 5, sc in next 2 tr, ch 5, tr in next 2 sc, ch 5, sc in next 2 tr. Ch 7, turn. Repeat 3rd and 4th rows for length desired. Fasten off.

No. 8883 . . . **Motif** . . . Ch 14, **1st row:** Sc in 2nd ch from hook, * ch 5, skip 1 ch, sc in next ch. Repeat from * across (6 loops). Ch 7, turn. **2nd, 3rd and 4th rows:** Sc in 1st loop, * ch 5, sc in next loop. Repeat from * across. Ch 7, turn. At end of 4th row do not ch or turn. Now working around outside of piece, make 4 sc in same loop as last sc, 3 sc in next loop, ch 3, 2 sc in same loop, 2 sc in each of next 5 sps, ch 3, 4 sc in next loop, 3 sc in next loop.

To make shamrock, ch 8, sc in 8th ch from hook, turn. In loop just made make sc, ch 1, (dc, ch 1) 6 times and dc, ch 1, sc at base of ch-8, ch 7, turn.

(Skip 2 sps, sc in next sp, ch 7) twice; sc in base of original ch-8, turn. In each loop make sc, ch 1, (dc, ch 1) 6 times and dc, ch 1, sc, sl st in ch-8 loop, turn. Sc in each st and each sp across shamrock. Make 3 sc in same loop on original piece, 4 sc in each of the next 2 loops, make another shamrock, 4 sc in each of the next 2 loops, 3 sc in next loop, make another shamrock, sc in same loop. Join and fasten off. Make a number of motifs and place them side by side to estimate desired length.

Heading . . . With right side of motif facing, attach thread in the 9th st (from base) of 1st shamrock. **1st row:** Ch 10, sc in 3rd ch from hook (p made), ch 3, p, ch 3, * sc in next ch-3 loop on same motif, (ch 3, p) twice; ch 3 (p loop made), sc in next ch-3 loop on same motif, make a p loop, dc in 9th st (from base) of next shamrock on same motif, make a p loop, dc in corresponding petal on shamrock of next motif, make a p loop. Repeat from * across, ending with p loop, dc in end petal of last shamrock. Ch 11, (p, ch 3) twice, turn. **2nd row:** * Sc between p's of next p loop, make a p loop. Repeat from * across ending with a p loop, tr at base of p loop. Ch 11, (p, ch 3) twice, turn. **3rd row:** * Sc between p's of next p loop, make a p loop. Repeat from * across, ending with d tr in 8th st of turning p loop. Ch 10, turn. **4th row:** Between the p's of next p loop make * dc, ch 4

and dc, ch 5. Repeat from * across, ending with ch 5, tr in 8th st of turning p loop. Fasten off.

No. 8896 . . . Measure off 2 inches on both sides of a corner and mark with pins. Draw a line diagonally across corner from pin to pin. Cut off corner. Roll this edge and whip down. Attach thread in 1st angle of corner. **1st rnd:** Work 49 sc's across to next angle. Now work a multiple of 14 plus 12 sc's from angle to next corner; make 3 sc's in corner. * Now work a multiple of 14 plus 7 sc's to next corner; make 3 sc's in corner. Repeat from * once more. Work a multiple of 14 plus 12 sc's to angle of corner. Join with sl st in 1st sc made. **2nd rnd:** Ch 1, sc in same place as sl st, sc in next 6 sc, (ch 3, skip 3 sc, in next sc make dc, ch 2 and dc, ch 3, skip 3 sc, sc in each of next 7 sc) 3 times. Ch 3, skip 1 sc, * in next sc make dc, ch 2 and dc, ch 3, skip 3 ch, sc in each of next 7 sc, ch 3, skip 3 sc. Repeat from * across to corner group of 3 sc; then ch 3, skip 1 sc, in center sc of corner make dc, ch 2 and dc, ch 3, skip 1 sc, * * sc in each of 7 sc, ch 3, skip 3 sc, in next dc make dc, ch 2 and dc, ch 3, skip 3 sc. Repeat from * * across to corner group of 3 sc. Turn corner as before. Then continue across to and around 3rd corner; then work in pattern to angle of corner ending with dc, ch 2 and dc in next to the last sc, ch 3, skip last sc, sl st in 1st sc made. **3rd rnd:** Ch 1, skip 1st sc, sc in next 5 sc, (ch 3, in next ch-2 sp make 4 dc with ch 2 between, ch 3, skip 1 sc, sc in next 5 sc) 3 times. Ch 3, * in next ch-2 sp make 4 dc with ch 2 between, ch 4, skip 2 sc, sc in next 3 sc, ch 4. Repeat from * across to corner; then ch 5, in corner ch-2 sp make 4 dc with ch 2 between. Ch 5, * * skip 2 sc, sc in next 3 sc, ch 4, in next ch-2 sp make 4 dc with ch 2 between, ch 4. Repeat from * * across to next corner. Turn corner as before. Then continue across to and around 3rd corner; work in pattern to angle of corner, ending with 4 dc with ch 2 between in last ch-2 sp, ch 3, sl st in 1st sc made.

Edge of handkerchief is now complete; work back and forth over the corner as follows: **1st row:** Ch 1, skip 1st sc, sc in next 3 sc, * ch 3, (dc in next dc, ch 2) twice; in center sp make 2 dc with ch 2 between, (ch 2, dc in next dc) twice; ch 3, skip 1 sc, sc in next 3 sc. Repeat from * 2 more times. Ch 1, turn. **2nd row:** Ch 1, skip 1 sc, sc in next sc, * ch 3, (dc in next dc, ch 2) 3 times; in center sp make 2 dc with ch 2 between, (ch 2, dc in next dc) 3 times; ch 3, skip 1 sc, sc in next sc. Repeat from * 2 more times. Fasten off. Turn and work over the center scallop only as follows: **3rd row:** Attach thread in 1st dc of center scallop, ch 5, to count as dc and ch 2, (dc in next dc, ch 2) 3 times; in center sp make dc, ch 2 and dc, (ch 2, dc in next dc) 4 times; ch 3, tr in 1st dc of next scallop, ch 2, turn. **4th row:** (Dc in next dc, ch 2) 4 times; in center sp make dc, ch 2 and dc, (ch 2, dc in next dc) 4 times; ch 2, holding back the last loop of each st on hook make dc in 3rd st of turning ch and tr in 1st dc of next scallop, thread over and draw through all loops on hook. Ch 5, turn. **5th row:** (Dc in next dc, ch 2) 5 times; in center sp make dc, ch 2 and dc, (ch 2, dc in next dc) 5 times, ch 2, dc in top of tr, ch 3, d tr in next dc on next scallop, ch 2, turn.

6th row: (Dc in next dc, ch 2) 6 times; in center sp make dc, ch 2 and dc, (ch 2, dc in next dc) 6 times; ch 2, holding back the last loop of each st on hook make dc in 3rd st of turning ch and d tr in next dc of next scallop, thread over and draw through all loops on hook. Fasten off. Turn and work picot edge as follows: **7th row:** Attach thread in 1st dc of 1st scallop, ch 6, sc in 3rd ch from hook (p made), (dc in next dc, p) 3 times; in center sp make dc, p and dc, (p, dc in next dc) twice; p, dc in same place as d tr, p, sc in top of d tr, (p, dc in next dc)

7 times; p, in center sp make dc, p and dc, (p, dc in next dc) 7 times; p, sc in top of d tr, p, dc in same place as d tr, (p, dc in next dc) twice; p, in center sp make dc, p and dc, (p, dc in next dc) 4 times. Fasten off.

●

No. 8895 . . . Starting at center of corner motif ch 7. Join with sl st to form ring. **1st row:** Ch 3, dc in ring, (ch 2, 2 dc in ring) 6 times; ch 2. Join with sl st in top st of starting chain. **2nd rnd:** Sl st in next dc, sl st in sp, ch 3, 4 dc in same sp, (ch 2, 5 dc in next sp) 6 times; ch 2. Join. **3rd rnd:** Ch 3 (to count as dc), holding back the last loop of each dc on hook make dc in each of next 2 dc, thread over and draw through all loops on hook (3-dc cluster made), * ch 2, holding back the last loop of each dc on hook make dc in same place as last dc, dc in each of next 2 dc, complete cluster as before, ch 5, make a cluster over the next 3 dc. Repeat from * around, joining last ch-5 with sl st in top of 1st cluster. Do not fasten off. Place this piece on handkerchief, having the center of crochet on point of a corner. Draw a line on handkerchief along curved edge of crochet. Cut off corner along this line, roll the edge and whip down. **4th rnd:** Sl st in sp, ch 5, dc in same sp, * ch 3, dc in center st of ch below, ch 3, in next ch-2 sp make dc, ch 2 and dc. Repeat from * around joining last ch-5 with sl st in 3rd st of starting chain. **5th**

rnd: Sl st in next sp, ch 3, 3 dc in same sp, (ch 3, skip 1 dc, dc in next dc, ch 3, in next ch-2 sp make 5 dc, ch 2 and 5 dc) 3 times; ch 3, skip 1 dc, dc in next dc, ch 3, 4 dc in next ch-2 sp. Fasten off.

Attach thread at left-hand angle of corner curve and work sc closely along rolled edge to next corner being sure to have a multiple of 15 plus 12 sc on this edge; work 3 sc in corner. * Work sc closely along next edge having a multiple of 15 plus 2 (not counting the 3 sc of corner); work 3 sc in corner. Repeat from * once more. Now work sc along remaining edge to right-hand angle of corner curve, having a multiple of 15 plus 12 sc. Work sc evenly along curve (no exact number needed). Join with sl st in 1st sc. **2nd rnd:** Ch 5, (skip 2 sc, dc in next sc, ch 2) twice; skip 3 sc, 2 dc in each of **next 2 sc,** * ch 2, skip 3 sc, dc in next sc, (ch 2, skip 2 sc, dc in next sc) twice, ch 2, skip 3 sc, 2 dc in each of next 2 sc. Repeat from * across to the 3-sc group at corner, ch 2, in center sc at corner make 3 dc with ch 2 between. Ch 2, skip 1 sc of corner, 2 dc in each of next 2 sc, * * ch 2, skip 3 sc, dc in next sc, (ch 2, skip 2 sc, dc in next dc) twice; ch 2, skip 3 sc, 2 dc in each of next 2 sc. Repeat from * * across to next corner. Turn corner as before. Work across 3rd edge same as 2nd edge, turn corner and **work across** 4th edge ending at right-hand angle of corner curve and being

Continued on page 45

35

A Bouquet of Edgings

Materials Required—AMERICAN THREAD COMPANY
"STAR" MERCERIZED TATTING COTTON
White or any Color desired

No. 3015

1—75 Yd. Ball will make 1¾ Yds. Edging.
Steel Crochet Hook No. 13 or 14.

Ch 5, d c in 1st ch, * ch 5, d c in d c, repeat from * for length desired.

2nd Row. Turn, sl st into 5 ch loop, ch 7, d c in next 5 ch loop, * ch 3, d c in next loop, repeat from * across row, turn.

3rd Row. Sl st to center of mesh * ch 5, sl st in 3rd st from hook for picot, ch 2, s c in next mesh, repeat from * across row, break thread.

No. 3016

1—75 Yd. Ball will make 1¼ Yds. of Edging.
Steel Crochet Hook No. 13 or 14.

Make a ch slightly longer than desired, d c in 8th st from hook, * ch 2, skip 2 chs, d c in next ch, repeat from * across row, turn.

2nd Row. * 3 s c in each of the next 2 meshes, ch 4, turn, d c in 1st s c, ch 2, d c in same space, ch 2, d c in same space, ch 4, turn, s c in 1st loop, ch 4, s c in same loop, s c in next loop, ch 4, s c in same loop, 4 s c over the ch 4 loop, sl st in top of next s c, repeat from * across row.

No. 3017

1—75 Yd. Ball will make 1¾ Yds. Edging.
Steel Crochet Hook No. 13 or 14.

Make a ch slightly longer than desired, turn, d c in 8th st from hook, ch 2, skip 2 chs, d c in next ch, ch 5, turn, sl st in top of 2nd d c, ch 1, turn, 7 s c over 4 ch loop, sl st in top of last d c, ch 2, skip 2 chs, d c in next ch, ch 4, turn, d c in center s c of scallop, ch 2, d c in same space, ch 2, d c in same space, ch 2, d c in same space, ch 4, d c in 6th st of ch, ch 1, turn, 7 s c over 4 ch loop, 3 s c in each of the next 3 loops, 7 s c over next loop, sl st in top of d c, * ch 2, skip 2 chs, d c in next ch, ch 2, skip 2 chs, d c in next ch, ch 5, turn, sl st in next d c, ch 1, turn and work 4 s c over loop, ch 4, sl st in top of s c for picot, 3 s c over same loop, sl st in top of d c, ch 2, skip 2 chs, d c in next ch, ch 2, skip 2 chs, d c in next ch, ch 2, skip 2 chs, d c in next ch, ch 5, turn, sl st in next d c, ch 1, turn and work 7 s c over loop just made, sl st in top of d c, ch 2, skip 2 chs, d c in next ch, ch 4, turn, 4 d c with ch 2 between each d c in center s c of small scallop, ch 4, sl st in next d c, ch 1, turn and work 7 s c over 4 ch loop, 3 s c in each of the next 3 loops, 7 s c over next 4 ch loop, sl st in top of d c, repeat from * across row.

No. 3018

1—75 Yd. Ball will make ¾ Yd. of Edging.
Steel Crochet Hook No. 13 or 14.

Make a ch slightly longer than desired, d c in 5th st from hook, * ch 1, skip 1 ch, d c in next ch, repeat from * across row, ch 3, turn.

2nd Row. Puff st in next mesh, ch 2, puff st in same mesh, (puff st: * thread over needle, insert in mesh, pull through, repeat from *, thread over needle and pull through all loops on needle but one, thread over and pull through 2 loops) ** ch 1, d c in next mesh, * ch 1, d c in next mesh, repeat from *, ch 1, 2 puff sts with ch 2 between in next mesh, repeat from ** across row ending with the 2 puff sts.

3rd Row. Sl st to 2 ch loop between puff st and work a puff st, ch 2, puff st in same space, * ch 2, skip 1 mesh, d c in next mesh, ch 1, d c in next mesh, ch 2, skip 1 mesh, puff st in next mesh, ch 2, puff st in same mesh, repeat from * across row.

4th Row. Sl st to 2 ch loop between puff sts and work puff st, ch 3, puff st in same space, ch 2, skip 1 mesh, d c in next mesh, ch 2, skip 1 mesh, puff st, ch 3, puff st between next 2 puff sts and continue in same manner across row.

5th Row. Sl st to ch between puff sts, * puff st in same space, ch 4, sl st in top of puff st for picot, ch 2, repeat from * twice, * ch 4, sl st in d c, ch 4, sl st in same space for picot, ch 4, and in ch between puff sts work 3 puff sts with a picot on top of each puff st, working ch 2 between puff sts, repeat from * across row.

No. 3019

1—75 Yd. Ball will make ¾ Yd. Edging.
Steel Crochet Hook No. 13 or 14.

Ch 5, d c in 1st st of ch, * ch 5, d c in d c, repeat from * for length desired.

2nd Row. Sl st to center of loop, ch 5, s c in next loop, ch 9, tr c in 4th st from hook, ch 3, sl st in top of tr c for picot, tr c in same space, ch 4, sl st in same st as 1st tr c, * ch 4, tr c in same st as last petal, ch 3, sl st in top of tr c for picot, tr c in same space, ch 4, sl st in same space, repeat from *, ch 5, ** skip 1 loop, s c in next loop, ch 5, s c in next loop, ch 9, tr c in 4th st from hook, ch 1, join to p of previous petal, ch 1, complete picot, tr c in same st of ch 9, ch 4, sl st in same st, * ch 4, tr c in same space, p, tr c in same space, ch 4, sl st in same space, ch 5, repeat from ** across row.

No. 3020

1—75 Yd. Ball will make 1½ Yds. of Edging.
Steel Crochet Hook No. 13 or 14.

Make a ch slightly longer than desired, d c in 8th st from hook, * ch 2, skip 2 chs, d c in next ch, repeat from * across row, turn.

2nd Row. Sl st into mesh, ch 5, d c in same mesh, * ch 1, d c in next mesh, ch 1, d c, ch 3, d c in next mesh, repeat from * across row, turn.

3rd Row. Sl st into loop, ch 7, sl st in 4th st from hook for picot, ch 4, sl st in same space for picot, ch 4, sl st in same space for picot, * ch 3, skip 1 d c, s c in next d c, ch 3, d c in next 3 ch loop, ch 4, sl st in top of d c for picot, ch 4, sl st in same space for picot, ch 4, sl st in same space for picot, repeat from * across row.

Directions for Nos. 3021, 3022 and 3023 on page 46

3015

3016

3017

3018

3019

3020

3021

3022

3023

Scalloped Edgings

EDGING (left)

MATERIALS:

CLARK'S O.N.T. or J. & P. COATS BEST SIX CORD MERCERIZED CROCHET, *size 30, in any color.*

Milward's Steel Crochet Hook *No. 10 or 11.*

FIRST MOTIF . . . Starting at center, ch 8, join with sl st to form a ring. **1st rnd:** Ch 5 (to count as d c and ch-2), * d c in ring, ch 2. Repeat from * until 8 sps are made; join last ch 2 with sl st to 3rd st of ch-5 first made (9 sps). **2nd rnd:** Sl st in sp, ch 3, 4 d c in same sp; make 5 d c in each sp around; join with sl st to top of ch 3. **3rd rnd:** Ch 3, d c in next 4 d c, * ch 3, d c in next 5 d c. Repeat from * around, ending with ch 3, join with sl st to top of ch-3 first made. **4th rnd:** Ch 3, d c in sl st, * d c in next 3 d c, 2 d c in next d c, ch 5, 2 d c in next d c. Repeat from * around, ending with ch 5, join to top of ch-3. **5th rnd:** Ch 3, * d c in each d c, holding back the last loop of each d c on hook; thread over and draw through all loops on hook (a cluster made); ch 7, s c in sp, ch 7. Repeat from * around, join last ch-7 to tip of 1st cluster made. Fasten off.

SECOND MOTIF . . . Work as for First Motif to 4th rnd incl. **5th rnd:** Ch 3 and complete a cluster as before, ch 7, s c in sp, ch 3, s c in loop to the right of a cluster on First Motif, ch 3, make next cluster on Second Motif, ch 3, skip cluster, and make s c in next loop on First Motif, ch 3, s c in next sp on Second Motif, ch 3, s c in next loop on First Motif, ch 3, make 3rd cluster on Second Motif, ch 3, skip cluster, and make s c in next loop on First Motif, ch 3, s c in next sp on Second Motif, ch 7, and complete rnd as for First Motif. Make necessary number of mo-

tifs, joining as 2nd was joined to 1st.

HEADING . . . 1st row: Attach thread to 5th loop preceding 1st joining, ch 7, s c in 3rd st from hook (p), ch 2, ch-3 p, ch 1, s c in next loop. * (Ch 1, ch-3 p, ch 2, ch-3 p, ch 1, s c in next loop) twice; (ch 1, ch-3 p, ch 2, ch-3 p, ch 1, d c in next free loop) twice; ch 1, ch-3 p, ch 2, ch-3 p, ch 1, s c in next loop. Repeat from * across, ending with d c in 5th free loop of last motif. Ch 7, turn. **2nd row:** S c in 3rd ch from hook (p) ch 2, ch-3 p, ch 1, s c between p's of next loop; * ch 1, ch-3 p, ch 2, ch-3 p, ch 1, s c between p's of next loop. Repeat from * across. Ch 5, turn. **3rd row:** D c in s c, * ch 2, between p's of next loop make d c, ch 2 and d c. Repeat from * across. Fasten off.

SCALLOPS . . . Attach thread to 6th loop preceding 1st joining, make 5 s c in loop, * in each of next 3 loops make (2 s c, ch 3) 3 times and 2 s c; 2 s c in next loop, ch 3, 2 s c in same loop, ch 5, turn; in center ch-3 of next loop make d c, ch 5 and d c; ch 5, make s c in center ch-3 of next loop, turn. In each of next 3 loops make (2 s c, ch 3) 3 times and 2 s c; ch 1, make 2 s c in incompleted loop, ch 3, 2 s c in same loop. In next loop make (2 s c, ch 3) 3 times and 2 s c; in next 2 loops make 5 s c. Repeat from * across. Fasten off.

EDGING (center)

MATERIALS:

CLARK'S O.N.T. or J. & P. COATS BEST SIX CORD MERCERIZED CROCHET, *size 50, in any color.*

Milward's Steel Crochet Hook *No. 12.*

Make a chain 7 inches long. **1st row:** D c in 8th ch from hook, (ch 2, skip 2 ch, d c in next ch) twice; ch 4, skip

3 ch, s c in next 4 ch, ch 8, skip 6 ch, s c in next 4 ch, ch 5, skip 4 ch, d c in next 5 ch. Ch 8, skip 4 ch, s c in next ch. Ch 3, turn. Hereafter, pick up only the back loop of each s c in s c-groups throughout. **2nd row:** 16 d c in loop, * ch 3, skip 4 d c, d c in next d c, ch 4, skip 1 s c, s c in next 2 s c, ch 4, skip 3 ch, s c in next 2 ch, ch 4, skip 1 s c, s c in next 2 s c, ch 4, skip 1 sp, 5 d c in next sp, ch 2, skip 1 sp, in next sp make d c, ch 2 and d c. Ch 3, turn. * **3rd row:** * In 1st sp make s c, ch 3 and s c; ch 2, skip 1 sp, s c in next d c, ch 3, skip 3 d c, s c in next d c, ch 8, skip 1st s c-group, s c in ch preceding next s c-group, s c in 2 s c, s c in next ch, ch 8, skip next s c-group, and ch-4, make 5 d c in next sp. * (Ch 1, skip 1 d c, d c in next d c) 8 times. Ch 2, skip 4 ch of foundation chain, s c in next ch. Ch 5, turn. **4th row:** D c in 1st sp, (ch 2, d c in next sp) 8 times. * Ch 3, skip 4 d c, d c in next d c, ch 4, skip 3 ch, s c in next 2 ch, ch 4, skip 1 s c, s c in next 2 s c, ch 4, skip 3 ch, s c in next 2 ch, ch 4, 5 d c in next sp, ch 2, skip 1 sp, in next sp make d c, ch 2 and d c. Ch 3, turn. * **5th row:** * In ch-2 sp make s c, ch 3 and s c; ch 3, skip 1 sp, s c in next d c, ch 3, skip 3 d c, s c in next d c, ch 4, s c in ch preceding 1st s c-group, s c in 2 s c, s c in next ch, ch 8, skip next s c-group, s c in ch preceding next s c-group, s c in 2 s c, s c in next ch, ch 5, 5 d c in next sp, * (ch 2, d c in next sp) 9 times. Ch 2, skip 3 ch of foundation chain, s c in next ch. Ch 3, turn. **6th row:** 3 d c in each of 10 sps, then repeat between *'s of 2nd row.

7th row: Repeat between *'s of 3rd row, then (ch 3, d c between 3rd and 4th d c) 10 times; ch 3, skip 3 ch of foundation chain, s c in next ch. Ch 3,

Continued on page 43

Handkerchief Trio

No. 16—
HANKY EDGE AND MEDALLION

WIDTH—1½ inches.

MATERIALS—Lily Six Cord Mercerized Crochet Cotton, size 50.

Finish linen with a rolled hem.

ROSE MEDALLION—Ch 6, dc in starting st, (ch 2, dc in same st) 6 times, ch 2, sl st in 3d ch st from 1st dc.

2nd Row—(1 sc, ch 2, 3 dc, ch 2 and 1 sc) over each 2-ch space.

3rd Row—Sl st to center of next petal, * ch 7, sc in 5th st from hook for a p, (ch 6, p) twice, ch 3, sc in center of next petal. Repeat from * 7 times. Fasten off.

4th Row—Join to center p of one p-loop, * ch 7, p, ch 8, p, (ch 7, p) twice, ch 2, sl st in center st between 3d and 4th ps from hook, ch 6, p, ch 3, sc in center p of next p-loop. Repeat from * 7 times. Fasten off.

5th Row—Join to tip of one p-loop, (ch 20, sc in next p-loop) 8 times. Fasten off. Baste Medallion about ¾ inch in from one corner. Cut out linen ¼-inch inside, turn this edge back, slashing as necessary, and baste down. With embroidery cotton, work satin stitch around over edge of crochet and linen. Cut away excess edge of linen on back.

EDGE—Make a Medallion thro Row 3. Make a 2d Medallion until 6 p-loops of 3d Row are completed. * Ch 7, p, ch 4, join with a sl st to center p on one p-loop of 1st Medallion, ch 2, sk last 2 sts of 4-ch, sc in next st, ch 6, p, ch 3, sc in next petal. Repeat from *, joining to next p-loop on 1st Medallion.

Fasten off. Continue to make and join Medallions into a straight row,—about 12 for each side of Hanky. Join these strips at corners, following illustration. Tack Medallions to edge of linen with neat over-and-over stitches, running thread along thro rolled hem between joinings.

2nd Row—Join to 1st of 3 p-loops on right-hand Medallion at one corner, * (ch 7, p, ch 8, p, ch 7, p, ch 7, p, ch 2, sl st in center st between 3d and 4th ps from hook, ch 6, p, ch 3, sc in next p-loop) twice, ch 7, p, ch 6, p, ch 3, dc down into corner joining of Medallions, ch 7, p, ch 6, p, ch 3, sc in next p-loop. Repeat from *. ** ch 7, p, ch 8, p, (ch 7, p) twice, ch 2, sl st between 3d and 4th ps from hook, ch 6, p, ch 3, sc in next p-loop, ch 7, p, ch 6, p, ch 3, dc in joining of Medallions, ch 7, p, ch 6, p, ch 3, sc in next p-loop. Repeat from ** around, making each corner like 1st one. Fasten off.

No. 17—HANKY EDGE & CORNER

MATERIALS—Lily Six Cord Mercerized Crochet Cotton, size 50.

Measure off 2¾ inches on both sides of one corner. Fold back corner and cut on diagonal line. Make a rolled hem, then work closely over all edges with sc. Fasten off. Mark center of diagonal corner line. With work wrong-side-up, join to 8th sc to right of mark, ch 6, tr in marked st, ch 11, tr in same st, ch 6, sl st in next 8th st. Ch 1, turn, 7 sc over 6-ch, 13 sc over 11-ch, 7 sc over 6-ch, sl st in next 7 sc. Turn, (ch 3, tr in next 2d sc on shell) 13 times, ch 3, sk 6 sc on linen, sl st in next 4 sc. Ch 3, turn, sc in last 3-ch space, (ch 5, sc in next space) 13 times, ch 3, sl st

in next 3d sc. Turn, (ch 5, sc in next 5-ch loop) 13 times, ch 3, sl st in same sc on linen. Ch 1, turn, (1 sc, 1 hdc, 3 dc, 1 hdc and 1 sc) over each 5-ch space. Sl st in next 9 sc on linen. Turn, (ch 7, sc in 5th st from hook for a p, ch 3, tr in center dc of next scallop) 14 times, ch 7, p, ch 3, sk 8 sc on linen, sl st in next 9 sc. Turn, (ch 8, p, ch 4, tr in next tr) 14 times, ch 8, p, ch 4, sk 7 sc on linen, sl st in each sc to corner. Turn, (ch 10, tr in next tr) 14 times, ch 10, sl st in corner of linen. Ch 1, turn, 11 sc over each 10-ch space.

EDGE—(Ch 6, sc in next 5th sc) repeated around.

2nd Row—Sl st to center of 1st loop, (ch 6, sc in next loop) repeated around. Make 5-ch loops around curve of lace corner.

3rd Row—(1 sc, 1 hdc, 3 dc, 1 hdc and 1 sc) over each loop. Fasten off.

No. 18—HANKY EDGING

WIDTH—½ inch.

MATERIALS—Lily Six Cord Mercerized Crochet Cotton, size 50.

EDGE—Finish edge of linen with a rolled hem. Join ⅛ inch to right of one corner, ch 13, sc ⅛ inch to left of corner, (ch 13, sc about 7/16 inch away) repeated around, making all corners like 1st one.

2nd Row—Ch 1, sc in next loop, * (ch 5, sc in same loop) 3 times, ch 3, sc in next loop. Repeat from * around.

3rd Row—Ch 1, sc in 1st loop, * ch 2, dc in next (center) loop, (ch 5, sc in 5th st from hook for a p, ch 1, dc in same loop) 3 times, ch 2, sc in next loop, ch 2, sc in next 5-ch loop. Repeat from * around. Fasten off.

Edgings for Sheets and Pillowcases

Compliment your guests with ensembles of fine bed linen, lavish with these intricate new crocheted designs, in snowy white, or in the soft, muted pastels that are so enchanting!

Use

Clark's O.N.T. or J. & P. Coats Mercerized Crochet, sizes 30 to 50.
J. & P. Coats Tatting Cotton.

No. 8223

Two-color edging — suggest Dark Lavender and Mid-Pink.

To begin, with Dark Lavender make a chain slightly longer than desired length, turn. **1st row:** D c in 8th ch from hook, * ch 2, skip 2 ch, d c in next ch. Repeat from * across. Ch 1, turn. **2nd row:** S c in 1st d c, * 2 s c in sp, s c in next d c. Repeat from * across. Ch 3, turn. **3rd row:** D c in each of next 2 d c, * ch 2, skip 4 s c; in next s c make: 2 d c, ch 2, 2 d c, ch 2, 2 d c (shell); ch 2, skip 4 s c, d c in each of next 3 s c. Repeat from * across, ending row with d c in last 3 s c. Break off. With right side of 3rd row toward you, attach Mid-Pink in 1st d c, s c to 1st d c of shell, s c in next d c, s c in next ch, * ch 3, s c in next ch, s c in each of next 2 d c, s c in next ch. Repeat from * once. S c across to next shell and continue in this manner across.

No. 8206

Suggest Self-shading color.

To begin, make a chain slightly longer than desired length, turn. **1st row:** D c in 8th ch from hook, * ch 2, skip 2 ch, d c in next ch (sp). Repeat from * across, having an even number of sps on row, turn. **2nd row:** Ch 5 (to count as d c and ch-2), * skip 2 ch of sp, d c in next d c, 2 d c in sp, d c over next d c (bl). Ch 2 and repeat from * across. Ch 3, turn. **3rd row:** Skip 1st bl, * 2 d c in next sp, ch 2, 2 d c in same sp (a shell). Skip next bl and repeat from * across. Ch 3, turn. **4th row:** 2 d c under first ch-2, ch 2, 2 d c under same ch-2, s c between 1st and 2nd shells of previous row. Continue in this manner across. Break off.

No. 8219

Make hairpin lace for desired length. Break off. Attach thread at 1st loop of one side (taking care to keep twist), and ch 3 (to count as d c), 2 d c in same loop, * ch 2, 3 d c in same loop; insert hook through next 3 loops and make an s c (taking care to keep twist as before). Keeping twist throughout, make 3 d c in next loop. Repeat from * across. Attach thread at opposite side and, keeping twist as before, make s c loosely in each loop across. Break off.

No. 8294

To begin, make a chain slightly longer than desired length, turn. **1st row:** D c in 6th ch from hook, * ch 1, skip 1 ch, d c in next ch. Repeat from * across (sps divisible by 10). Ch 1, turn. **2nd row:** S c in 1st d c, * s c in sp, s c in d c. Repeat from * 3 more times, s c in next sp, ch 3, ** s c in next d c, s c in sp. Repeat from ** once more, s c in d c, turn. **3rd row:** Ch 10, sl st in 5th s c beyond ch-3. Ch 1, turn. **4th row:** 15 s c under ch-10 just made, s c in next sp of foundation, s c in next d c, turn. **5th row:** * Ch 2, skip 1 s c, d c in next s c. Repeat from * 6 more times, ch 2, skip 1 s c of foundation, sl st in next s c of foundation (8 sps), sl st in next 2 s c, turn. **6th row:** Ch 2, skip 2 sl st of foundation, d c in next s c, * ch 2, d c in next d c. Repeat from * across, ending row with ch 2, d c in next s c (9 sps), ch 2, s c in next d c of foundation row (10 sps in all), turn. **7th row:** Ch 8, skip 3 sps of scallop, d c in next d c, * ch 8, skip 2 sps, d c in next d c. Repeat from * once. Ch 8, skip 3 sps, sl st in next s c of foundation. Ch 1, turn. **8th row:** Under each ch-8 loop make: 5 s c, ch-5 p, 5 s c; s c in next s c of foundation. This completes one scallop. Hereafter, work 2nd scallop as for 1st scallop through 7th row. **8th row:** 5 s c under 1st ch-8 loop, ch 2, remove hook from loop, insert hook in corresponding picot in 1st scallop and draw loop through, ch 2 and complete 8th row as for 8th row of 1st scallop. Continue in this manner, joining each scallop to previous one as 2nd was joined to 1st.

No. 8205

To begin, make a chain slightly longer than desired length, turn. **1st row:** D c in 7th ch from hook, * ch 2, skip 2 ch, d c in next ch. Repeat from * across. Ch 3, turn. **2nd row:** D c in 1st sp, * ch 2, d c in next sp. Repeat from * across, d c in 3rd ch of turning ch-5. Ch 5, turn. **3rd row:** D c in 1st sp, * ch 2, d c in next sp. Repeat from * across, d c in turning ch-3. Work 2 s c in first 2 sps along short end, and 7 s c in 3rd sp. Do not break off but work scallops along foundation chain as follows: **Scallops. 1st row:** 3 s c in each of 4 sps, s c in next sp, turn. **2nd row:** Ch 6, s c in 5th s c, * ch 6, skip 4 s c, s c in next s c. Repeat from * once more (3 loops). Ch 1, turn. **3rd row:** 9 s c in each of next 2 sps, 4 s c in next sp (an incompleted loop), turn. **4th row:** Ch 6, sl st in 5th s c of center loop, ch 6, s c in 5th s c in 3rd loop. Ch 1, turn. **5th row:** In 1st loop, make 4 s c, ch 3, 4 s c; s c in next loop, turn. **6th row:** Ch 6, sl st in 5th s c of next loop (thus forming top loop of scallop). Ch 1, turn. **7th row:** In top loop, make 4 s c, ch 3, 4 s c. Working along incompleted loops of previous row, * make

8223
8206
8219
8294
8205
8260
8260
8204

Directions for No. 8204 on page 46

1 s c in next loop, ch 3, 4 s c in same loop. Repeat from * to complete remaining loop. Then make 3 s c in each of next 6 filet sps, and 1 s c in following sp, and continue scallops across, having 2 s c between scallops.

No. 8260

Edging. To begin, make a chain slightly longer than desired length, turn. **1st row:** D c in 8th ch from hook, * ch 2, skip 2 ch, d c in next ch. Repeat from * across. Ch 5, turn. **2nd row:** S c in 1st sp, * ch 5, s c in next sp. Repeat from * once more. Then ** ch 8, skip 1 sp, s c in next sp, ch 5, and make 5 ch-5 loops (as before) and repeat from ** across, ending row with 3 ch-5 loops. Ch 5, turn. **3rd row:** Make 3 ch-5 loops, * s c in same place as last s c, 3 s c in ch-8 loop, ch 3, 5 s c in same loop, ch 3, 3 s c in same loop, 2 s c in next loop. Then make 4 ch-5 loops. Repeat from * across, ending row with 3 ch-5 loops. Ch 5, turn. **4th row:** 3 ch-5 loops, * ch 8, s c in center s c between 2 p's, ch 8, s c in next loop, 3 ch-5 loops. Repeat from * across, ending row with 3 ch-5

loops. Ch 5, turn. **5th row:** 3 ch-5 loops, s c in same place as last s c, * into each of next 2 ch-8 loops make: 3 s c, ch 5, 5 s c, ch 5, 3 s c; then, 2 s c in next loop, ch 5, s c in next loop, ch 5, 2 s c in next loop. Repeat from * across, ending row with 3 ch-5 loops. Ch 5, turn. **6th row:** 3 ch-5 loops, * ch 8, s c in center s c of 1st ch-8 loop, ch 8, s c in center of next ch-8 loop, ch 8, s c in next loop, ch 5, s c in next loop. Repeat from * across, ending row with 3 ch-5 loops. Ch 1, turn. **7th row:** 4 s c in each of 3 ch-5 loops, * into each of next 3 ch-8 loops make: 3 s c, ch 5, 5 s c, ch 5, 3 s c; then, 4 s c in next loop. Repeat from * across. Break off.

Insertion. Work exactly as for edging (1st to 7th rows incl.). Ch 5, turn. **8th row:** * S c in center s c of next loop, ch 3. Repeat from * until 3 loops are made, ch 3, ** s c in next ch-5, ch 3. Repeat from ** 5 times, ch 4, s c in next ch-5, ch 3, and continue in this manner across. Ch 5, turn. **9th row:** Skip 1 ch, d c in next ch, * ch 2, skip 2 sts, d c in next st. Repeat from * across. Break off. Attach thread to end of foundation ch and work to correspond with opposite side, starting with the 2nd row.

41

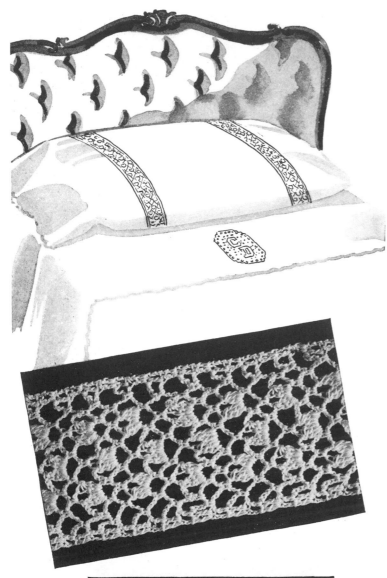

Monograms for Your Bed Linens

INSERTION

**Materials Required—AMERICAN THREAD COMPANY
"STAR" or "GEM" MERCERIZED CROCHET
COTTON, Size 20, White**

1 125-yd. Ball will make ½ yd. of insertion.
Steel Crochet Hook No. 12.

Ch 30 and work 1 d c in 4th st from hook, * ch 5, skip 4 chs, s c in next ch, repeat from * 3 times, ch 5, skip 4 chs, 1 d c in each of the next 2 chs, ch 3, turn.

2nd Row—D c in next d c, ch 4, s c in next loop, ch 4, thread over needle, insert in next loop and work off 2 loops, thread over needle, insert in same space and work off 2 loops, thread over needle, insert in same space and work off 2 loops twice, thread over needle and work off all remaining loops (cluster st), ch 3, cluster st in same loop, ch 4, s c in next loop, ch 4, cluster st in next loop, ch 3, cluster st in same loop, ch 4, s c in next loop, ch 4, d c in d c, d c in 3rd st of ch, ch 3, turn.

3rd Row—D c in d c, ch 4, skip 1 loop, s c in next loop, ch 4, s c in next loop between the 2 cluster sts, ch 4, s c in next loop, ch 4, s c in next loop, ch 4, s c between next 2 cluster sts, ch 4, s c in next loop, ch 4, skip 1 loop, d c in d c, d c in 3rd st of ch.

4th Row—Ch 3, turn, d c in d c, * ch 4, s c in next loop, repeat from * twice, ch 4, cluster st in next loop, ch 3, cluster st in same loop, * ch 4, s c in next loop, repeat from * twice, ch 4, d c in d c, 1 d c in 3rd st of ch.

5th Row—Ch 3, turn, d c in d c, ch 4, skip 1 loop, s c in next loop, ch 4, 2 cluster sts with ch 3 between in next loop, ch 4, skip 1 loop, s c between next 2 cluster sts, ch 4, skip 1 loop, 2 cluster sts with ch 3 between in next loop, ch 4, s c in next loop, ch 4, skip 1 loop, d c in d c, 1 d c in 3rd st of ch, ch 3, turn.

6th Row—D c in d c, ch 4, s c in next loop, ch 4, skip 1 loop, s c in loop between next 2 cluster sts, ch 4, s c in next loop, ch 4, s c in next loop, ch 4, s c in loop between next 2 cluster sts, ch 4, skip 1 loop, s c in next loop, ch 4, d c in d c, d c in 3rd st of ch, ch 3, turn.

7th Row—D c in d c, ch 4, skip 1 loop, s c in next loop, ch 4, s c in next loop, ch 4, 2 cluster sts with ch 3 between in next loop, ch 4, s c in next loop, ch 4, s c in next loop, ch 4, skip 1 loop, d c in d c, 1 d c in 3rd st of ch, ch 3, turn.

8th Row—D c in d c, ch 4, s c in next loop, ch 4, 2 cluster sts with ch 3 between in next loop, ch 4, skip 1 loop, s c in loop between next 2 cluster sts, ch 4, skip 1 loop, 2 cluster sts with ch 3 between in next loop, ch 4, s c in next loop, ch 4, d c in d c, 1 d c in 3rd st of ch, ch 3, turn and repeat from 3rd row for length desired.

INITIAL C-D

**Materials Required—AMERICAN THREAD COMPANY
"STAR" or "GEM" MERCERIZED CROCHET
COTTON, Size 30, White**

Steel Crochet Hook No. 12 or 13.

Ch 29, d c in 8th st from hook, * ch 2, skip 2 chs, d c in next ch, repeat from * 6 times.

2nd Row—Ch 7, turn, * d c in d c, 2 d c in mesh, repeat from * 7 times, d c in 3rd st of ch, ch 2, thread over needle 3 times, insert in same space as last d c and work off all loops 2 at a time.

3rd Row—Ch 7, turn, 4 d c in mesh, 8 o m, 1 s m, ch 2, d tr c in same st as last d c, ch 8, turn and work back and forth according to illustration. Finish with a row of s c all around.

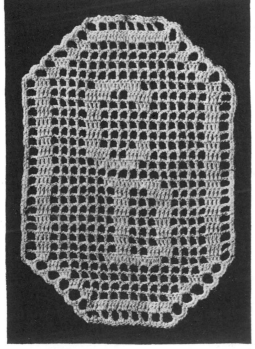

INITIAL B

Materials Required—AMERICAN THREAD COMPANY "STAR" or "GEM" MERCERIZED CROCHET COTTON, Size 30, White

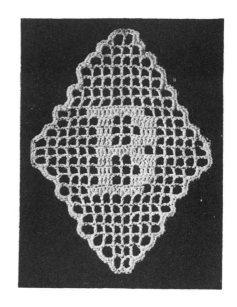

Steel Crochet Hook No. 12 or 13.
"Star Twist" for Sewing.

Ch 11, d c in 8th st from hook, ch 2, skip 2 chs, d c in next ch, ch 7, turn.

2nd Row—D c in d c, ch 2, d c in next d c, ch 2, skip 2 chs, d c in next ch, ch 2, d tr c in same space, ch 7, turn.

3rd Row—D c in d tr c, * ch 2, d c in next d c, repeat from * twice, ch 2, skip 2 chs, d c in next ch, ch 2, d tr c in same space, ch 7, turn and work back and forth according to illustration. Finish with a row of s c all around.

Baste motif in position on right side and sew firmly. Cut the material from under side, allowing enough material for a very narrow hem, turn hem under and sew again securely.

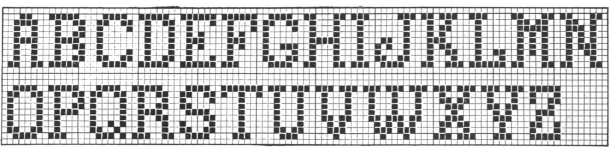

Scalloped Edgings
Continued from page 38

turn. **8th row:** 4 d c in each of 11 sps, then repeat between *'s of 4th row. **9th row:** Repeat between *'s of 5th row, then (ch 3, d c between 4th and 5th d c) 11 times; ch 3, skip 3 ch of foundation chain, s c in next ch. Ch 3, turn. **10th row:** 5 d c in each of 12 sps, then repeat between *'s of 2nd row. **11th row:** Repeat between *'s of 3rd row, then (ch 4, d c between 5th and 6th d c) 12 times; ch 4, skip 4 ch of foundation chain, s c in next ch. Ch 1, turn. **12th row:** 5 s c in each of 13 sps, then repeat between *'s of 4th row. **13th row:** Repeat between *'s of 5th row, then (ch 6, s c between 5th and 6th s c) 13 times; ch 6, skip 4 ch of foundation chain, s c in next ch. Ch 5, turn. **14th row:** S c in 1st loop, (ch 6, s c in next loop) 13 times; then repeat between *'s of 2nd row. **15th row:** Repeat between *'s of 3rd row, then (ch 6, s c in next loop) 13 times; ch 6, skip 3 ch of foundation chain, s c in next ch. Ch 3, turn. **16th row:** Skip 2 ch, * in next ch make (s c, ch 5) 3 times and s c; ch 5, skip 2 ch of next loop. Repeat from * 6 more times. (Ch 6, s c in next loop) 7 times; then repeat between *'s of 4th row. **17th row:** Repeat between *'s of 5th row, then ch 8, s c in next loop. Ch 3, turn. Repeat 2nd to 17th rows incl. for desired length, joining end of every other row with s c, to corresponding loop of previous scallop.

EDGING *(right)*

MATERIALS:

J. & P. COATS KNIT-CRO-SHEEN, *in any color.*

Milward's Steel Crochet Hook *No. 7.*

Starting at one narrow end, ch 12. Join with sl st. **1st row:** 20 s c in ring. Join with sl st to 1st s c made. Turn. **2nd row:** Ch 3, skip 1 s c, s c in next s c (a loop made). Repeat from beginning of row until 5 loops in all are made. Turn. **3rd row:** Sl st in 1st loop, ch 4, 3 tr in same loop, holding back on hook the last loop of each tr, thread over and draw through all loops on hook (a cluster made), * ch 5, 4 tr in next loop, holding back on hook the last loop of each tr and complete cluster as before. Repeat from * 3 more times. Ch 1, turn. **4th row:** 5 s c in each of 4 sps, s c in tip of last cluster (21 s c in row). Ch 5, turn. **5th row:** Skip next s c, d c in next s c, ch 2. Repeat from beginning of row across, ending with d c in last s c. Ch 1, turn. **6th row:** 2 s c in next sp, s c in next d c. Repeat from beginning of row across, ending with s c in 3rd st of turning ch (30 s c in row). Ch 4, turn. **7th row:** 5 d c in next s c, drop loop from hook, insert hook in chain preceding the 5 d c and draw dropped loop through (pc st made), * ch 3, skip 1 s c, pc st in next s c. Repeat from * across (15 pc sts in row). Turn. **8th row:** Ch 3, s c in next sp. Repeat from beginning of row until 7 loops in all are made, ch 10, s c in next sp. Turn. **9th row:** 15 s c in ch-10 loop, s c in next loop. Turn. **10th row:** Sl st in next s c, s c in next s c, (ch 3, skip 1 s c, s c in next s c) 5 times. Turn. Repeat 3rd to 10th rows incl. for desired length, ending with the 7th row. Do not break off, but work along one long side as follows:

HEADING . . . 1st row: Ch 11, skip pc st and next sp, 3 d tr in next s c, holding back on hook the last loop of each d tr; 3 d tr in first free ch-3 loop, holding back on hook the last loop of each d tr, skip 2 loops, 3 d tr in next loop, holding back on hook the last loop of each d tr, thread over and draw through all loops on hook; ch 8, skip 1 loop, d c in next loop, ch 3, s c in next loop, ch 3, d c in tip of pc st. Repeat from * across. Ch 1, turn. **2nd row:** 3 s c in next 2 sps, 5 s c in next sp, ch 5, 5 s c in next sp. Repeat from beginning of row across. Ch 4, turn. **3rd row:** Skip 1 s c, d c in next s c, ch 1. Repeat from beginning of row across. Fasten off.

43

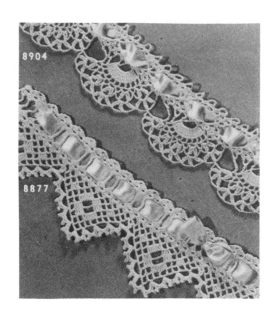

Beadings and Corners

PRETTY BEADINGS

ON LAMPSHADES,

LOVELY LINGERIE,

CORNERS ON LINENS

No. 8904 . . . Starting at narrow end, ch 18. **1st row:** 2 dc in 8th ch from hook, ch 2, 2 dc in next ch, ch 5, skip 7 ch, 2 dc in next ch, ch 2, 2 dc in next ch. Ch 7, turn. **2nd row:** In next ch-2 sp make 2 dc, ch 2 and 2 dc (shell over shell), ch 5, shell over shell. Ch 7, turn. **3rd row:** Shell over shell, ch 3, sc over both chains below, ch 3, shell over shell. Ch 7, turn. **4th and 5th rows:** Shell over shell, ch 5, shell over shell. Ch 7, turn. **6th row:** Shell over shell, ch 3, sc over both chains below, ch 3, shell over shell. Ch 10, do not turn but work sc in next loop on this side; ch 4, tr in next loop on this side. Turn. **7th row:** Make 18 tr in ch-10 loop, ch 1, shell over shell, ch 5, shell over shell. Ch 7, turn. **8th row:** Shell over shell, ch 5, shell over shell, ch 1, dc in next tr, (ch 2, skip next tr, dc in next tr) 8 times; ch 2, dc in top st of ch-4, tr tr in next loop on this side. Ch 5, turn. **9th row:** Sc in next ch-2 sp, (ch 5, sc in next ch-2 sp) 8 times; ch 3, shell over shell, ch 3, sc over both chains below, ch 3, shell over shell. Ch 7, turn. **10th row:** Shell over shell, ch 5, shell over shell, ch 1, * holding back the last loop of each tr on hook make 2 tr in next ch-5 loop, thread over and draw through all loops on hook (cluster made), ch 5, cluster in same loop, ch 3, sc in next loop, ch 3. Repeat from * 3 more times; in next loop make cluster, ch 5 and cluster. Ch 9, turn. **11th row:** (In next ch-5 sp make 3 clusters with ch 5 between) 5 times; ch 3, shell over shell, ch 5, shell over shell. Ch 7, turn. **12th to 17th rows incl:** Repeat 3rd, 4th and 5th rows respectively, twice. **18th to 21st rows incl:** Repeat 6th to 9th rows incl. **22nd row:** Same as 10th

row, ending with ch 4, sc in top of center cluster of adjoining 3-cluster group. Ch 4, turn. **23rd row:** Repeat 11th row. Repeat last 12 rows (12th to 23rd rows incl) for length desired. Fasten off.

No. 8877 . . . Starting at narrow end, ch 17. **1st row:** 2 dc in 4th ch from hook, ch 2, 3 dc in next ch (shell made), ch 5, skip 7 ch, 3 dc in next ch, ch 2, 3 dc in next ch (shell), ch 2, skip 2 ch, dc in next ch. Ch 5, turn. **2nd row:** Dc in 1st dc of shell, ch 2, in ch-2 sp of shell below make 3 dc, ch 2 and 3 dc (shell over shell), ch 5, shell over shell. Ch 3, turn. **3rd row:** Shell over shell, ch 5, shell over shell, ch 2, skip 2 dc, dc in next dc (sp made), ch 2, dc in next dc, ch 2, dc in 3rd st of turning ch (2 more

sps made). Ch 5, turn. **4th row:** Dc in next dc (sp made), 2 dc in sp, dc in next dc (bl made), ch 2, dc in next dc, ch 2, shell over shell, ch 5, shell over shell. Ch 3, turn. **5th row:** Shell, ch 5, shell, 5 sps. Ch 5, turn. **6th row:** Make 2 sps, 2 bls, 1 sp, ch 2, shell, ch 5, shell. Ch 3, turn. **7th row:** Shell, ch 5, shell, 2 sps, 1 bl, ch 4, skip 5 dc, dc in next dc, 1 bl, 1 sp. Ch 5, turn. **8th row:** 1 sp, 1 bl, ch 4, dc in next dc, 1 bl, 2 sps, ch 2, shell, ch 5, shell. Ch 3, turn. **9th row:** Shell, ch 5, shell, 2 sps, 1 bl, 2 sps, 5 dc over ch-4, 2 sps. Ch 5, turn. **10th row:** Make 10 sps, shell, ch 5, shell. Ch 3, turn. **11th row:** Shell, ch 5, shell, ch 2, skip 2 dc, dc in next dc. Ch 5, turn. Repeat last 10 rows (2nd to 11th rows) for length desired. Fasten off.

Edging . . . 1st row: Attach thread

Continued on next page

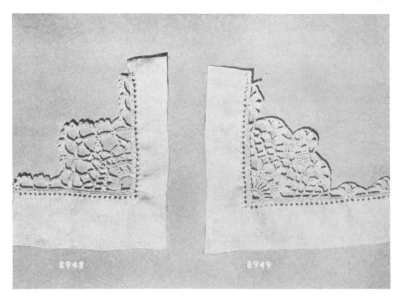

in end sp (next to shell) on scalloped edge, ch 10, * skip 1 sp, sc in next sp, (ch 7, skip 1 sp, sc in next sp) 3 times; (ch 7, sc in next sp) twice; (ch 7, skip 1 sp, sc in next sp) 3 times; ch 3, skip 1 sp, holding back the last loop of each tr on hook make tr in each of the next 2 sps, thread over and draw through all loops on hook, ch 3. Repeat from * across. Ch 1, turn. **2nd row:** In each ch-7 loop make (3 sc, ch 3, sc in 3rd ch from hook) twice and 3 sc; make 3 sc over each ch-3 loop. Fasten off.

●

No. 8949 . . . Corner . . . Ch 10, join with sl st to form ring. **1st row:** Ch 1, 7 sc in ring. Ch 5, turn. **2nd row:** (Tr in next sc, ch 1) twice; tr in same place as last tr, (ch 1, tr in next tr) 3 times. Ch 3, turn. **3rd row:** (Dc in next sp, dc in tr) 3 times; in next sp make dc, ch 3 and dc, (dc in next tr, dc in sp) 3 times; dc in 4th st of turning ch. Ch 8, turn. **4th row:** Skip 4 dc, holding back the last loop of each tr on hook make 3 tr in 5th dc, thread over and draw through all loops on hook (cluster made), ch 5, cluster in same place as last cluster, in ch-3 sp make 3 clusters with ch 5 between, skip 3 dc, in next dc make cluster, ch 5 and cluster, ch 3, tr in top st of turning ch. Ch 7, turn. **5th row:** Sc in next loop, (ch 5, sc in next loop) 5 times; ch 3, dc in 5th st of turning ch. Ch 7, turn. **6th row:** Sc in next loop, (ch 5, sc in next loop) twice; ch 3, in next loop make 3 dc, ch 3 and 3 dc, ch 3, (sc in next loop, ch 5) twice; sc in next loop, ch 3, dc in 4th st of turning ch. Ch 7, turn. **7th row:** Sc in next loop, (ch 5, sc in next loop) twice; ch 3, dc in next 3 dc, in next sp make 2 dc, ch 3 and 2 dc, dc in next 3 dc, ch 3, (sc in next loop, ch 5) twice; sc in next loop, ch 3, dc in 4th st of turning ch. Ch 7, turn. **8th row:** Sc in next loop, ch 5, sc in next loop, ch 3, in next loop make cluster, ch 5 and cluster, ch 3, dc in 5 dc, in sp make 2 dc, ch 3 and 2 dc, dc in 5 dc, ch 3, skip next loop, in next loop make cluster, ch 5 and cluster, ch 3, sc in next loop, ch 5, sc in next loop, ch 3, dc in 4th st of turning ch. Fasten off.

Cut fabric close to hemstitching (about 1/16 inch). Attach thread and work 2 sc in each hole to angle of corner; work only 1 sc in each of the 3 holes at corner. Continue thus until sc has been worked in entire hemstitching. Fasten off. Sew crocheted corner in place.

Edging . . . With right side facing attach thread in end sc, ch 1, sc in same place where thread was attached, * ch 3, skip 6 sc, in next sc make 3 clusters with ch 3 between, ch 3, skip 6 sc, sc in next sc. Repeat from * across, ending with ch 3, skip 6 sc, sc in 1st loop of crocheted corner. Ch 3, skip 2 loops on corner, in next loop (between clusters) make 3 clusters with ch 3 between, ch 3, skip 3 dc, sc in next dc, ch 3, in next sp make 3 clusters with ch 3 between, ch 3, skip 3 dc, sc in next dc, ch 3, skip next loop, in next loop make 3 clusters with ch 3 between, ch 3, sc in last loop, ch 3, skip 6 sc on hemstitching, in next sc make 3 clusters with ch 3 between. Continue thus along edge. Fasten off.

●

No. 8948 . . . Corner . . . Ch 13. Join with sl st to form ring. **1st row:** Ch 7, holding back the last loop of each tr on hook, make 3 tr in ring, thread over and draw through all loops on hook (cluster made), in same ring make ch 3, cluster, ch 5, cluster, ch 3, cluster, ch 3 and tr. Ch 1, turn. **2nd row:** 3 sc in each of next 2 sps, in next sp make 3 sc, ch 3 and 3 sc, 3 sc in each of next 2 sps. Ch 1, turn. **3rd row:** Sc in 1st sc, ch 4, (skip 1 sc, dc in next sc, ch 1) 4 times, ch 1, in next loop make dc, ch 1 and dc; ch 1, dc in next sc, (ch 1, skip 1 sc, dc in next sc) 4 times. Ch 8, turn. **4th row:** Skip 1 sp, sc in next sp, ch 8, skip 1 sp, sc in next sp, ch 5, skip 1 sp, in next sp make dc, ch 5 and dc; ch 5, skip 1 sp, sc in next sp, ch 8, skip 1 sp, sc in next sp, ch 4, skip 1 st of turning ch, tr in next ch. Ch 9, turn. **5th row:** Holding back the last loop of each tr on hook make tr in each of first 2 loops, thread over and draw through all loops on hook (a joined tr made), ch 5, work a joined tr as before over next 2 loops, ch 5, tr in same loop where last tr was made, ch 5 and work over other half to correspond, ending with ch 5, tr in center st of last loop. Ch 1, turn. **6th row:** 6 sc in each of next 3 ch-5 loops, ch 5, 6 sc in each of remaining 3 ch-5 loops. Fasten off.

Cut fabric close to hemstitching (1/16 inch). Attach thread, 2 sc in each hole to angle of corner; work only 1 sc in each of 3 holes at corner. Continue thus until sc has been worked in entire hemstitching. Fasten off. Sew crocheted corner in place.

Edging . . . 1st row: With wrong side facing attach thread in end sc, ch 1, sc in same place where thread was attached, * ch 7, skip 5 sc, sc in next sc. Repeat from * across to 6 sc from edge of crocheted corner, ch 3, skip 5 sc, tr in next sc, ch 3, sc over joined tr's, ch 7, sc over next joined tr's, ch 7, in center loop make dc, ch 7 and dc, (ch 7, sc over next joined tr's) twice; ch 3, tr in next sc on hemstitching, ch 3, * * skip 5 sc, sc in next sc, ch 7. Repeat from * * to end. Ch 1, turn. **2nd row:** In each ch-7 loop make (2 sc, ch 3) 3 times and 2 sc; work 5 sc in each ch-3 loop at both sides of crocheted corner. Fasten off.

Delicate Touches
No. 8895 . . .
Continued from page 35

sure end of row corresponds with beginning of row. Sl st in starting chain of 5th row of corner motif. **3rd rnd:** Ch 3, holding back the last loop of each dc on hook make dc in next 3 dc, complete cluster as before, (ch 3, dc in next dc, ch 3, 5-dc cluster over next 5 dc, ch 3, 5 dc in ch-2 sp, ch 3, 5-dc cluster over next 5 dc) 3 times; ch 3, dc in next dc, ch 3, 3-dc cluster over next 3 dc, ch 3, sl st in last dc on motif, sl st in 3rd st of ch-5 on edge of handkerchief. Sl st in sp, ch 5, dc in next sp, * ch 5, make a 4-dc cluster over next 4 dc, ch 5, skip next dc, dc in next sp, ch 2, dc in next sp. Repeat from * around, joining last dc with sl st in top of 1st cluster.

4th rnd: Ch 4, dc in next dc, ch 5, dc in next cluster, ch 5, (5-dc cluster over next 5 dc, ch 5, dc in next cluster, ch 5, dc in next dc, ch 5, dc in next cluster, ch 5) twice; 5-dc cluster over next 5 dc, ch 5, dc in next dc, ch 5, dc in next dc, tr in last cluster, * ch 2, dc in next ch-2 sp, ch 2, dc in next ch-5 sp, ch 7, skip next cluster, dc in next sp. Repeat from * around, joining last ch 2 with sl st to top st of starting chain. **5th rnd:** * Ch 3, in next sp make dc, ch 3, sc in 3rd ch from hook (p made) and dc, ch 3, sc in next sp, ch 3, in top of cluster make dc, p and dc, ch 3, sc in next sp, ch 3, in next sp make dc, p and dc, ch 3, sc in next dc. Repeat from * 2 more times; ch 2, skip next sp, sc in next sp, * * ch 3, in center st of ch-7 loop make (dc, p) twice and dc, ch 3, sc in next dc, ch 2, sc in next sp. Repeat from * * to corner, make a p shell in center dc of corner. Then continue around. Join and fasten off. Sew remaining edge of motif to sc edge on curve of corner.

45

A Bouquet of Edgings

Continued from page 36

No. 3021

Materials Required—AMERICAN THREAD COMPANY "STAR" MERCERIZED TATTING COTTON
White or any Color desired

1—75 Yd. Ball will make 20 inches of Edging.

Steel Crochet Hook No. 13 or 14.

Ch 6, 2 d c in 5th st from hook, ch 2, 2 d c in same space, ch 4, turn.

2nd Row. 2 d c in ch 2 loop, ch 2, 2 d c in same space, ch 7, turn, s c in ch 4 loop of previous row, ch 1, turn and work 11 s c over loop just made, ch 2, 2 d c, ch 2, 2 d c in center of shell, ch 4, turn, 2 d c, ch 2, 2 d c in center of shell, ch 7, turn, s c in loop of previous row, ch 1, turn and work 6 s c over loop just made, ch 15, sl st in 7th st from hook to form a ring, ch 5, turn, d c in ring, * ch 3, d c in ring, repeat from * 3 times, ch 5, sl st in ring, ch 1, turn and work 1 s c, 4 d c, 1 s c over first mesh of flower, s c in next mesh, 2 d c in same mesh, join to center st of 1st scallop, 2 d c, 1 s c over same mesh, 1 s c, 4 d c, 1 s c in each of the next 4 meshes of flower, 11 s c over ch for stem, 5 s c over remainder of previous loop, ** ch 2, 2 d c, ch 2, 2 d c in center of shell, ch 4, turn, 2 d c, ch 2, 2 d c in center of shell, ch 7, turn, s c in ch 2 loop with last scallop, ch 1, turn and work 11 s c over ch just made, ch 2, 2 d c, ch 2, 2 d c in center of shell, ch 4, turn, 2 d c, ch 2, 2 d c in center of shell, ch 7, turn, s c in loop with last scallop, ch 1, turn and work 6 s c over ch just made, ch 15, sl st in 7th ch from hook to form a ring, ch 5, turn, d c in ring, * ch 3, d c in ring, repeat from * 3 times, ch 5, sl st in ring, ch 1, turn, 1 s c, 4 d c, 1 s c in next mesh, 1 s c, 2 d c in next mesh, skip the half scallop, join in center s c of next scallop, 2 d c, s c in same mesh of flower, 1 s c, 2 d c in next mesh, join to center st of stem of previous flower, 2 d c, s c in same mesh, 1 s c, 4 d c, 1 s c in each of the next 3 meshes, 11 s c over ch for stem, 5 s c over remainder of previous scallop, repeat from ** for length desired.

No. 3022

1—75 Yd. Ball will make 34 inches of Edging.

Steel Crochet Hook No. 13 or 14.

Ch 12, 2 d c in 7th st from hook, ch 2, 2 d c in same space, ch 4, skip 4 chs, 2 d c, ch 2, 2 d c in next ch, ch 5, turn.

2nd Row. D c in 2 ch loop, ch 4, sl st in top of d c just made for picot, 4 d c in same space, ch 2, d c, p, d c in same space, ch 2, d c, p, d c in same space, 2 d c in 5 ch loop, ch 2, 2 d c in same loop, ch 2, 2 d c in next 2 ch loop, ch 2, d c in end loop, ch 6, turn.

3rd Row. 2 d c, ch 2, 2 d c in 1st loop, ch 4, skip next loop, 2 d c, ch 2, 2 d c in next loop, (center of shell) ch 5, turn and repeat 2nd and 3rd rows for length desired.

No. 3023

1—75 Yd. Ball will make 26 inches of Edging.

Steel Crochet Hook No. 13 or 14.

Ch 8, join to form a ring, ch 5, s c in ring, 5 d c in same ring, (petal) ch 5, s c in same space, ch 6, turn.

2nd Row. S c in next loop, ch 4, s c in 2nd st of petal, ch 4, s c in center d c of petal, ch 4, s c in end loop, ch 5, turn.

3rd Row. S c in next loop, 5 d c in same loop, s c in same loop, ch 3, 1 s c, 5 d c, 1 s c in next loop, ch 4, s c in next loop, ch 4, s c in next loop, ch 6, turn.

4th Row. S c in next loop, ch 4, s c in next loop, ch 4, s c in center st of petal, ch 4, s c in center st of next petal, ch 4, s c in next loop, ch 5, turn.

5th Row. S c in next loop, ch 4, 1 s c, 5 d c, 1 s c in next loop, ch 4, s c in next loop, ch 4, s c in next loop, ch 4, s c in next loop, ch 6, turn.

6th Row. S c in next loop, ch 4, s c in next loop, ch 4, s c in center st of petal, ch 4, s c in next loop, ch 4, s c in next loop, ch 4, s c in next loop, ch 6, turn.

7th Row. Sl st in 4th st from hook for picot, ch 2, s c in next loop, * ch 6, sl st in 4th st from hook for picot, ch 2, s c in next loop, repeat from * twice, * ch 4, s c in next loop, repeat from * twice, ch 6, turn.

8th Row. S c in next loop, ch 4, s c in next loop, ch 4, s c in next loop, ch 5, turn.

9th Row. S c, 5 d c, 1 s c in next loop, ch 4, s c in next loop, ch 4, s c in next loop, ch 6, turn.

10th Row. S c in next loop, ch 4, s c in next loop, ch 4, s c in center st of petal, ch 4, s c in end loop, ch 5, turn.

11th Row. 1 s c, 5 d c, 1 s c in next loop, ch 3, 1 s c, 5 d c, 1 s c in next loop, ch 4, s c in next loop, ch 4, s c in next loop, ch 6, turn.

12th Row. S c in next loop, ch 4, s c in next loop, ch 4, s c in center st of next petal, ch 4, s c in center st of next petal, ch 4, s c in end loop, ch 5, turn.

13th Row. S c in next loop, ch 4, 1 s c, 5 d c, 1 s c in next loop, * ch 4, s c in next loop, repeat from * twice, ch 6, turn.

14th Row. S c in next loop, ch 4, s c in next loop, ch 4, s c in next loop, ch 4, s c in center st of petal, ch 4, s c in next loop, ch 4, s c in next loop, ch 4, s c in next loop at end of previous petal, ch 4, s c in next loop at end of single petal, ch 6, turn.

15th Row. Sl st in 4th st from hook for picot, ch 2, s c in next loop, * ch 6, sl st in 4th st from hook for picot, ch 2, s c in next loop, repeat from * 3 times, ch 4, s c in next loop, ch 4, s c in next loop, ch 4, s c in next loop, ch 6, turn and repeat from the 8th row for length desired.

Edgings for Sheets and Pillowcases

No. 8204

Shown on page 41

Edging. Make a chain slightly longer than the length desired. **1st row:** D c in 4th ch from hook, * ch 1, skip 1 ch, d c in next ch. Repeat from * across. Ch 4, turn. **2nd row:** * D c in next ch-1 sp, ch 1. Repeat from * until 3 sps are made, ** ch 7, skip 3 sps, d c in next sp, make 5 more sps as before. Repeat from ** across, ending row with 3 sps. Ch 1, turn. **3rd row:** S c in each d c and in each ch-1 sp, then into ch-7 loop make: 1 s c, 1 half d c, 2 d c, 1 tr, 3 d tr, 1 tr, 2 d c, 1 half d c, 1 s c. Repeat from * across. Ch 5, turn. **4th row:** * D c in 2nd d c of ch-7 loop, ch 5, skip tr, d c in next d tr, ch 5, skip 1 d tr, d c in next d tr, ch 5, skip tr, d c in next d c, ch 5, skip 4 s c, s c in each of next 3 s c, ch 5. Repeat from * across, ending row with s c in last s c. Ch 1, turn. **5th row:** * 6 s c in next loop, into each of next 3 loops make: 3 s c, ch 5, s c in 5th ch from hook (1 p made), 3 s c; then, 6 s c in next loop, s c in center s c of 3-s c group. Repeat from * across. Break off.

Insertion. Work exactly as for edging (1st to 5th rows incl.). Break off. **6th row:** Attach thread to 1st p made, * ch 5, s c in next p. Repeat from * across. Break off. Attach thread to 1st sp of foundation row, and work to correspond with opposite side. Break off.

BEDSPREADS

Arrow and Rose

MATERIALS:

J. & P. COATS KNIT-CRO-SHEEN

SINGLE SIZE

27 balls of White or Ecru,
or 43 balls of any color.

DOUBLE SIZE

38 balls of White or Ecru,
or 60 balls of any color.

Steel crochet hook No. 7.

GAUGE: 4 bls or sps make 1 inch; 4 rows make 1 inch. Each strip measures 13½ inches wide. For a single size spread about 67½ x 107 inches, make 5 strips. For a double size spread about 94½ x 107 inches, make 7 strips.

Directions on page 70

Southern Hospitality

No. 3408
Materials Required—
AMERICAN THREAD COMPANY
"PURITAN" MERCERIZED CROCHET
AND KNITTING COTTON

67 300-yd. Balls White, Ecru, Cream or Beige.

Steel Crochet Hook No. 8 or 9.

Each Motif measures about 6 inches.

234 Motifs are required for spread measuring about 84 x 108 inches without the fringe.

MOTIF. Ch 7, join to form a ring, ch 5, d c in ring, * ch 2, d c in ring, repeat from * 9 times, ch 2, join in 3rd st of ch 5.

2nd Row—Ch 3, 3 d c in same space, drop loop off hook, insert hook in 3rd st of ch and pull loop through, (popcorn st) * ch 3, 4 d c popcorn st in next d c, repeat from * 10 times, ch 3, join in 1st popcorn st.

3rd Row—Ch 6, d c in 4th ch from hook, * d c in next popcorn st, ch 4, d c in first ch, repeat from * all around, join.

4th Row—Ch 3, 2 d c in same space, * ch 5, 3 d c in next d c, repeat from * all around, ch 5, join in 3rd st of ch.

5th Row—Ch 5, * skip 1 d c, d c in next d c, ch 2, d c in center st of next loop, ch 2, d c in next d c, ch 2, repeat from * all around ending with skip 1 d c, d c in next d c, ch 2, d c in center st of next loop, ch 2, join in 3rd st of ch 5.

6th Row—Ch 3 and work a popcorn st in same space, * ch 3, popcorn st in next d c, repeat from * all around, ch 3, join.

7th Row—Sl st into loop and work a popcorn st in each loop with ch 4 between popcorn sts, ch 4, join.

8th Row—Work 4 s c over each loop, join.

9th Row—Ch 6, d c in 4th st from hook, * skip 2 s c, d c in next s c, ch 4, d c in 1st st of ch, repeat from * all around, join.

10th Row—Ch 5, 3 d c in next d c, ch 2, * 1 d c in next d c, ch 2 3 d c in next d c, ch 2, repeat from * all around, join in 3rd st of ch 5.

11th Row—Ch 4, skip 1 d c, d c in next d c, ch 3, sl st in top of d c for picot, ch 4, * skip 1 d c, s c in next d c, ch 4, d c in center d c of next group, picot, ch 4, repeat from * all around.

Work a second motif joining to first motif in last row as follows, ch 4, skip 1 d c, d c in next d c, ch 1, join to picot of 1st motif, ch 1, complete picot, * ch 4, skip 1 d c, s c in next d c, ch 4, skip 1 d c, d c in next d c, ch 1, join to next picot of 1st motif, ch 1, complete picot, repeat from * once and finish row same as 1st motif.

Join 3rd motif to 2nd motif and join 4th motif to 3rd and 1st motifs in same manner leaving 3 picots free between joining to fill in with joining motif.

Work 230 more motifs having 3 rows of 15 motifs, 8 rows of 18 motifs, (adding all rows on one side for shaping at lower edge) and 3 rows of 15 motifs.

Joining Motif. Work first 2 rows of large motif, ch 7 d c in next popcorn st, * ch 4, d c in next popcorn st, repeat from * all around, ch 4, join.

Next Row—Ch 4, join to first free picot of large motif, ch 1, sl st in 3rd st of ch to complete picot, * ch 4, s c in next loop of small motif, ch 4, d c in next d c, ch 1, join to next free picot of large motif, ch 1, complete picot, repeat from * until all 12 picots have been joined, break thread.

Tassel Fringe. Over an 8 inch cardboard, wind thread 20 times, cut one end, loop over joined picots between motifs, draw ends through loop and tighten. * Over a 7 inch cardboard, wind thread 20 times, cut one end, loop through next loop before the picot, draw ends through loop and tighten, repeat from * once. * Over a 6 inch cardboard, wind thread 20 times, cut one end, loop through next loop before the picot, draw ends through and tighten. Repeat from * 4 times, then repeat 7 inch tassel twice.

At the 2 corners have 2 7-inch tassels, 10 6-inch tassels and 2 7-inch tassels.

Cluny Filet Bedspread

Approximate Size: 86 inches by 101 inches.

MATERIALS: Bucilla Wondersheen (mercerized) Cotton, Article 3666, 25 skeins,

or

Bucilla Blue Label (delustered) Cotton, Article 3457, 22 skeins.

Bucilla Steel Crochet Hooks, Sizes 7 and 9, Article 4300.

Gauge: Each square when finished should measure 7½ inches.

Filet—4 spaces = 1 inch,　　4 rows = 1 inch.

LACE SQUARE—With fine (size 9) hook, ch 5, join with a slip st into a ring. **1st round:** work 8 s c in ring, join with a slip st in first s c of round. **2nd round:** ch 6, work 1 d c in next st, ch 3 and 1 d c in each st of round, end with ch 3, join with a slip st in 3rd st of chain 6 at beginning of round. **3rd round:** ch 5, * work 1 treble (twice over hook) in next space, 1 d c in same space, 1 s d c (s d c—short d c—thread over hook, draw up a loop in place, thread over and through all 3 loops on hook) in same space, 1 s c in same space, 1 s c in top of next d c, work a group of 1 s c, 1 s d c, 1 d c and 1 treble,—all in

52

next space, 1 treble in top of next d c; repeat from * around, join with a slip st in top of chain 5 at beginning of round. **4th round:** ch 1, 1 s c in joining st of round below, * ch 5, skip 4 sts, work a long treble (3 times over hook) in next st, ch 5, 1 d c in center of long treble just made, ch 5, skip the next 4 sts, 1 s c in next st; repeat from * around, end with ch 5, join with a slip st in first s c of round. **5th round:** work 5 s c in first space, ch 5, slip st in 5th st from hook (picot), ch 5, a 2nd picot, ch 5, a 3rd picot, slip st in last s c made (triple picot), * work 5 s c in next (corner) space, work a triple picot and 5 more s c in same space, a triple picot and 5 s c in each of the next 2 spaces; repeat from * around, working all corners' alike, end with 5 s c in last space, join with a slip st in first s c of round, ch 5, picot, ch 2, draw up a loop in joining st, draw up a loop in next st, thread over and through one loop 3 times in succession, thread over and through 2 loops, over and through one loop twice in succession, over and through remaining 2 loops on hook, thus joining round with a triple picot. **6th round:** ch 1, work 1 s c in top of last triple picot made, ch 5, 1 s c in center picot of next triple picot, * ch 5, 1 d c in center picot of next (corner) triple picot, ch 5, 1 more d c in same place, ch 5 and 1 s c in center picot of each of the next 3 triple picots; repeat from * around, end with ch 5, join with a slip st in first s c of round. **7th round:** ch 9, work a long treble in 7th st from hook, ch 7, slip st in same st (petal at beginning of round), ch 7, thread 3 times over hook, draw up a loop in 7th st from hook, thread over and through 2 loops 3 times in succession; retaining the last 2 loops on hook, thread 3 times over hook, draw up another loop in same st, over and through 2 loops 3 times in succession, over and through remaining 3 loops on hook, ch 5, picot, ch 7, slip st in same st (regular petal), slip st in each of the next 2 sts, work 5 s c in each of the next 2 spaces, 9 s c in next (corner) space, 5 s c in each of the next 2 spaces, * ch 9, work a petal st in 7th st from hook, ch 7, a 2nd petal in 7th st from hook, ch 7, work a 3rd petal in 7th st from hook, slip st in each of the remaining 2 chain sts (a triple petal), 5 s c in each of the next 2 spaces, 9 s c in next corner space, 5 s c in each of the next 2 spaces; repeat from * twice, then slip st in each of the 2 slip sts of first petal, ch 7, work a petal in 7th st from hook, slip st in same place as the first petal of round, ch 7, slip st in top st of ch 7 at beginning of round, ch 3, 1 s c in top of first petal. **8th round:** ch 9, work 1 s c in picot of next petal, * skip the next 7 sts, work a long treble in next st, ch 9, skip the next 6 sts, 1 s c in next st, ch 9, skip the next 6 sts, a long treble in next st, 1 s c in picot of next petal, ch 9 and a s c in picot of each of the next 2 petals; repeat from * around, end with ch 9, join with a slip st in first st of round. **1st row of band:** work 11 s c in next space, 1 s c in next s c, 1 s c in top of next long treble, 11 s c in next space, 1 s c in next s c, 11 s c in next space, 1 s c in top of next long treble, 1 s c in next s c, 11 s c in next space. **2nd row of band:** ch 1, turn, 1 s c in first st, * ch 1, skip 1 st, 1 s c in next st; repeat from * across to end of row below. **3rd row of band:** ch 1, turn, 1 s c in first st, 1 s c in next space, ch 1 and 1 s c in each space to end of row, then work 1 s c in last s c. **4th row of band:** ch 1, turn, 1 s c in first st, ch 1 and 1 s c in each space to end of row, ch 1, skip 1 st, 1 s c in last st. **5th row of band:** ch 1, turn, work 1 s c in first st, 1 s c in next space, ch 1 and 1 s c in each of the next 16 spaces.

1st row of scallop: ch 3, turn, skip 4 spaces, work a long treble in next space, ch 3, a 2nd long treble in same space, ch 3 and a 3rd long treble in same space, ch 3 and a 4th long treble in same space,

ch 3, skip 4 spaces, work a slip st in next s c, slip st in each of the next 4 sts. **2nd row of scallop:** turn, ch 5, picot, work 1 d c in first space of scallop, * ch 5, picot, 1 d c in top of next long treble, ch 5, picot, 1 d c in next space; repeat from * 3 times, ch 5, picot, thread twice over hook, draw up a loop in last s c worked in 5th row, thread over and through 2 loops, draw up a loop in next space in 4th row, thread over and through 2, over and through 2, draw up a loop in next space in 4th row, over and through remaining 3 loops on hook, ch 1 and 1 s c in each of the next 2 spaces. **3rd row of scallop:** ch 3, turn, work 1 d c in top of first d c in scallop, ch 3 and 1 d c in top of each d c below, ch 3, skip 2 spaces in 5th row, slip st in next s c. **Point row:** turn, work 3 s c in first space on scallop, * 1 s c in top of next d c, 3 s c in next space; ch 1, turn, skip 1 st, 1 s c in each of the next 6 sts; ch 1, turn, skip first st, 1 s c in each of the next 5 sts, ch 1, turn, skip first st, 1 s c in each of the next 4 sts; ch 1, turn, skip first st, 1 s c in each of the next 3 sts; ch 1, turn, skip first st, 1 s c in each of the next 2 sts; ch 1, turn, skip first st, 1 s c in next st; slip st down side of point just made (1 st to each row), work 1 s c in top of next d c below, 3 s c in next space on scallop, then repeat from * until there are 5 points completed, ending with the slip sts down side of last point, 1 s c in next space in 4th row of scallop, ch 1 and 1 s c in each of the next 2 spaces, 1 s c in next st. **5th row of scallop:** ch 8, turn, work 1 s c in tip of first point, * ch 4, work a long treble in s c left free between the next 2 points, ch 4, 1 s c in tip of next point; repeat from * 3 times, ch 8, work 1 s c in last st in 5th row. **6th row of scallop:** ch 1, turn, work 11 s c in first space, 1 s c in next s c, * 6 s c in next space, 1 s c in top of next long treble, 6 s c in next space, 1 s c in next s c; repeat from * 3 times, then work 11 s c in last space. **7th row of scallop:** same as 2nd row of scallop. **8th row of scallop:** same as 3rd row of band. **9th row of scallop:** same as 4th row of band; fasten off thread. Make a loop on hook, working from right side of last **round** on square, work 11 s c in first free space, then continue to work a 2nd scallop on this side of square following the directions for first scallop, beginning with the 1st row of band. Continue in same way to work a scallop on each of the remaining 2 sides of square, do not fasten off thread after the 4th scallop is completed. **9th round:** ch 1, turn, work 1 s c in first st, * 1 s c in next space, ch 1 and 1 s c in each space to end of scallop, 1 s c in next st, 1 s c in first st of next scallop; repeat from * around, thus connecting the 4 scallops, join with a slip st in first st of round, slip st in each of the next 8 sts. **10th round:** ch 8, * skip 1 space, work a d c in next space, ch 3, skip 1 space, 1 s d c in next space, ch 3, skip next space, 1 s c in next space, ch 3, skip next space, 1 s c in next space, ch 3, skip 1 space, 1 s d c in next space, ch 3, skip next space, 1 d c in next space, ch 3, skip next space, 1 treble in next space, ch 3, skip 1 space, work a long treble in next **stitch**, ch 5, 1 d c in center of long treble just made, ch 3, skip 1 space, 1 treble in next space, ch 3, skip next space, 1 d c in next space, ch 3, skip 1 space, 1 s d c in next space, ch 3, skip next space, 1 s c in next space, ch 3, skip 1 space, 1 s c in next space, ch 3, skip 1 space, 1 s d c in next **space**, ch 3, **skip next space**, 1 d c in **next space**, ch 3, skip next space, 1 treble in next space, ch 3, thread 3 times over hook, skip 1 space, draw up a loop in next space, thread over and through 2 loops on hook, thread over, skip **the next 8 stitches**, draw up a loop in next space, thread over and through 2, over and through 3, over and through 2, over and through remaining 2 loops on

Continued on page 54

Cluny Filet Bedspread

Continued from page 53

hook (a decreasing treble), ch 3, skip next space, work a treble in next space, ch 3; repeat from * around, thus working a corner on each scallop, end with a decreasing treble, ch 3, join with a slip st in 5th st of chain 8 at beginning of round. **Final round:** * work a group of 4 s c in next space, 5 s c in next space; repeat from * 3 times, 9 s c in next (corner) space, * 4 s c in next space, 5 s c in next space; repeat from last * 8 times, then work this corner like last. In this way continue to work around, being careful to work all corners alike. Join with a slip st in first s c and fasten off thread. This completes one square, make 72 of these squares.

FILET SQUARE—With coarse (size 7) hook, ch 93, work 1 d c in 9th st from hook (A on chart on page 14), * ch 2, skip 2 sts, 1 d c in next st (a space); repeat from * to end of chain (29 spaces in row). **2nd row (see chart):** ch 5, turn, work 1 d c in 2nd d c, ch 2 and 1 d c in top of each d c in row below, end with ch 2, 1 d c in 6th st of turning chain (29 spaces in row). **3rd row (see chart):** ch 5, turn, work 1 d c in 2nd d c below, ch 2 and 1 d c in top of next d c, 2 d c in next space, 1 d c in top of next d c, 2 d c in next space, 1 d c in top of next d c, 2 d c in next space, 1 d c in top of next d c (a group of 10 d c over 3 spaces—3 blocks), work 19 spaces over the next 19 spaces, a group of 10 d c over the next 3

spaces, ch 2, 1 d c in top of next d c, end with ch 2, 1 d c in 3rd st of turning chain below. **4th row (see chart):** ch 5, turn, work 1 d c in top of 2nd d c below, ch 2 and 1 d c in top of next d c, 1 d c in each of the next 3 sts, ch 2, skip 2 sts, 1 d c in each of the next 4 sts, work 19 spaces over the next 19 spaces, continue to follow chart to end of row. From now on continue to follow chart to end. **Edging:** working down side of square, work 5 s c around post of last d c made, 3 s c in each space to next corner, 9 s c in corner space, 3 s c in each space to next corner, work this corner same as last, then continue around, being careful to have all corners worked alike, end with 4 s c in same space as first 5 s c of round, join with a slip st in first s c of round and fasten off thread. This completes one filet square, make 71 of these squares.

Arrange squares in checker board fashion, 11 squares in width and 13 squares in length as shown on diagram on page 14. Sew from wrong side with an over-hand stitch, taking up top thread only on each edge and being careful to have seams as elastic as the crocheted fabric.

BORDER—With coarse (size 7) hook, working from right side, beginning in center st of corner space on a corner square, make 1 d c, ch 5, 1 more d c,—all in same st, * ch 2, skip 2 sts, 1 d c in next st; repeat from * to next corner of spread, work a group of 1 d c, ch 5, 1 d c,—all in center st of corner space, continue working in spaces as before to next corner, work this corner same as last, then continue around, working all corners alike, end with ch 2, join with a slip st in top of first d c of round and fasten off thread. **Point round:** working from right side, make a loop on hook, skip the corner space, work a slip st in next d c, ch 3, 1 d c in top of next d c (a half space at beginning of row), ch 2 and 1 d c in top of each of the next 6 d c, ch 2, thread over hook, draw up a loop in top of next d c, thread over and through 2 loops on hook, thread over, skip 2 sts, draw up a loop in top of next d c, thread over and through 2, over and through remaining 3 loops on hook (a half space at end of row); ch 3, turn, work a half space, 5 spaces, a half space; ch 3, turn, a half space, 3 spaces, a half space; ch 3, turn, a half space, 1 space, a half space, ch 3, turn, 1 d c in top of end d c, thus completing one point; fasten off thread. Skip one space on edge, work a 2nd point in same way as first point over the next 9 spaces. Continue in this way to work 3 points over each square on spread to within 1 space of corner space; skip the next 3 spaces (one space before corner, corner space, one space after corner), work in points along this side of spread in same way to next corner, ending the last point in space before corner, leave corner space free, then work along remaining 2 sides of spread in same way, being careful to have opposite corners worked alike. **Final round:** working from right side and beginning in first corner space, † work a group of 3 s c, ch 4, picot, 3 s c,—all in corner space, * 3 s c in each of the next 2 spaces up side of point, ch 4, picot, 3 s c in each of the next 2 spaces, ch 4, picot, 5 s c in point space, ch 4, picot, 5 more s c in same space, ch 4, picot, 3 s c in each of the next 2 spaces, ch 4, picot, 3 s c in each of the next 2 spaces, 1 s c in free space between points, ch 4, picot, 1 more s c in same space; repeat from * to next corner, work a group of 1 s c, ch 4, picot, 1 s c,—all in space just before corner, a group of 3 s c, ch 4, picot, 3 s c,—all in corner space, a group of 1 s c, ch 4, 1 s c,—all in next space, continue to work in picot edging along points of this side of spread to next corner, then repeat from † around, join with a slip st in first s c of round and fasten off thread. Darn in all ends neatly.

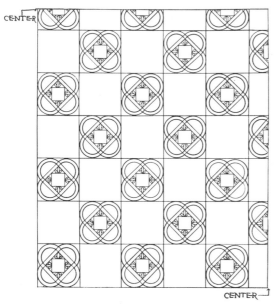

CENTER

CENTER

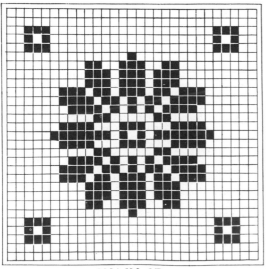

54

CHAIN 93   A

Star and Flower Bedspread

MATERIALS—Daisy Mercerized Crochet Cotton No. 20, (see Page 16 for color selection); No. 7 Hook.

Approximate size, 78x97½ inches, tassels extra.

FLOWER BLOCKS—Ch 9, join into a ring, (1 sc in ring, ch 24, 1 sl st in 1st st of 24-ch) 12 times. Fasten off.

2nd Row—Join to 1 loop, (ch 8, 1 sc in next loop) 12 times.

3rd Row—Ch 1, (9 sc over 8-ch, 1 sc in sc) 12 times, 1 sl st in starting 1-ch.

4th Row—(The sc around circle in this row are worked in back loops only.) Ch 1, 1 sc in 10 sc, (ch 22, sk last 3 ch sts, 1 sc in remaining 19 ch sts, 1 sc in next 15 sc) 7 times, ch 22, sk 3 sts, 1 sc in 19 ch sts, 1 sc in next 4 sc, 1 sl st in 1-ch at start of row, 1 sl st in back loops of next 2 sc.

5th Row—Ch 1, 1 sc in next 2 sc, * ch 4, 1 dtr in 3rd st up next petal vein, (ch 3, 1 dtr in next 3rd st) 3 times, ch 3, 1 tr in next 3rd st, ch 4, 1 sc in end of vein. Now, working down other side of vein, ch 4, 1 tr exactly opposite tr, (ch 3, 1 dtr opposite next dtr) 4 times, ch 4, sk 6 sc on circle, 1 sc in back loops of next 3 sc. Repeat from * around, fastening final 4-ch to 1-ch at start of row. 1 sl st in next sc.

6th Row—Ch 1, * 4 sc over next 4-ch, 1 sc in next st, (3 sc over next 3-ch, 1 sc in next st) 4 times, 4 sc over next 4-ch, 3 sc in back loop of next sc, 4 sc over 4-ch, 1 sc in next st, (3 sc over 3-ch, 1 sc in next st) 4 times, 4 sc over next 4-ch, 1 sl st in center sc between petals. Repeat from * around and join to first 1-ch. Fasten off.

7th Row—(The sc in this row are worked in back loops only.) Join to the 1st of 3 sc at tip of 1 petal, ch 1, 2 sc in next sc, * a 5-ch p in last sc, 1 sc in same st with last sc, 1 sc in next 3 sc, p, 1 sc in 5 sc, p, (4 sc, p) twice, 7 sc, sk 3 sc on next petal, 1 sc in next 4 sc, ch 1, remove hook, insert back in 4th of last 7 sc on previous petal, catch loop and pull through, ch 1, 1 sl st back in last sc, 4 sc, ch 2, remove hook, insert back in last p on previous petal, catch loop and pull through, ch 2, 1 sl st back in last sc, (4 sc, p) twice, 5 sc, p, 1 sc in 2 sc, 2 sc in next st. Repeat from * around and fasten off. Make 180 Flower Blocks.

STAR BLOCKS—SOLID POINTS—Ch 40, sk last 2 ch sts, 1 sc in next 18 sc, sk next 2 ch sts, 1 sc in remaining 18 sts. All the following rows are worked in the back loops only of sts of previous row. Ch 2, turn, 1 sc in the last 17 sc, sk 2 sc, 1 sc in next 17 sc, 1 sc in 2-ch at end of last row. Ch 2, turn, 1 sc in last 17 sc, ch 5, 1 sc in 1st st of 5-ch for a p, sk 2 sc, 1 sc in next 16 sc, 1 sc in 2-ch at end of row. Ch 2, turn, 1 sc in last 16 sc, sk p and next sc, 1 sc in 16 sc, 1 sc in 2-ch at end. Ch 2, turn, 16 sc, ch 5, 1 sc in 1st st for a p, sk 2 sc, 15 sc, 1 sc in 2-ch. Ch 2, turn, 15 sc, sk p and next sc, 15 sc, 1 sc in

2-ch. Ch 2, turn, 15 sc, a ch-5 p, sk 2 sc, 14 sc, 1 sc in 2-ch. Ch 2, turn, 14 sc, sk p and next sc, 14 sc, 1 sc in 2-ch. Ch 2, turn, 14 sc, sk 2 sc, 13 sc, 1 sc in 2-ch. Ch 2, turn, 13 sc, sk p and next sc, 13 sc, 1 sc in 2-ch. Ch 2, turn, 13 sc, a ch-5 p, sk 2 sc, 12 sc, 1 sc in 2-ch. Ch 2, turn, 12 sc, sk p and next sc, 12 sc, 1 sc in 2-ch. Ch 2, turn, 12 sc, p, sk 2 sc, 11 sc, 1 sc in 2-ch. Ch 2, turn, 11 sc, sk p and next sc, 11 sc, 1 sc in 2-ch. Ch 2, turn, 11 sc, p, sk 2 sc, 10 sc, 1 sc in 2-ch. Ch 2, turn, 9 sc, sk p and next 2 sc, 9 sc, 1 sc in 2-ch. Ch 2, turn, 9 sc, p, sk 2 sc, 8 sc, 1 sc in 2-ch. Ch 2, turn, 8 sc, sk p and next sc, 8 sc, 1 sc in 2-ch. Ch 2, turn, 8 sc, p, sk 2 sc, 7 sc, 1 sc in 2-ch. Ch 2, turn, 6 sc, sk p and next 2 sc, 6 sc, 1 sc in 2-ch. Ch 2, turn, 6 sc, p, sk 2 sc, 5 sc, 1 sc in 2-ch. Ch 2, turn, 4 sc, sk p and next 2 sc, 4 sc, 1 sc in 2-ch. Ch 2, turn, 4 sc, p, sk 2 sc, 3 sc, 1 sc in 2-ch. Ch 2, turn, 3 sc, sk p and next sc, 3 sc, 1 sc in 2-ch. Ch 2, turn, 3 sc, p, sk 2 sc, 1 sc in 2-ch. Ch 2, turn, 2 sc, sk p and next sc, 2 sc, 1 sc in 2-ch. Ch 2, turn, 2 sc, sk 2 sc, 1 sc in next, 1 sc in 2-ch. Ch 2, turn, 1 sc, sk 2 sc, 1 sc in next, 1 sc in 2-ch. Ch 2, turn, 1 sc, sk 2 sc, 1 sc in 2-ch. Fasten off. Make 2 Solid Points for Star Block.

LATTICE POINTS—Ch 36, 1 sc in 8th st from hook, (ch 4, 1 sc in next 3rd st) 3 times, ch 3, 1 sc in next 7th st, (ch 4, 1 sc in next 3rd st) 4 times. Ch 6, turn, 1 sc in last 4-ch loop, (ch 4, 1 sc in next loop) 3 times. 5 dc over next 3-ch loop, working these into a Popcorn st, 1 sc in next loop, (ch 4, 1 sc in next loop) 3 times, ch 4, 1 dc in same last loop. Ch 6, turn, 1 sc in last 4-ch loop, (ch 4, 1 sc in next loop) 3 times, ch 2, 1 sc in next, (ch 4, 1 sc in next) 3 times, ch 2, 1 dc in same last loop. Turn (ch 4, 1 sc in next 4-ch loop) 3 times, ch 1, a 5-dc Popcorn over next 2-ch loop, ch 1, 1 sc in next 4-ch loop, (ch 4, 1 sc in next loop) 3 times. Ch 6, turn, 1 sc in last 4-ch loop, (ch 4, 1 sc in next) twice, ch 2, 1 dc in top of Popcorn, ch 2, 1 sc in next loop, (ch 4, 1 sc in next) twice, ch 2, 1 dc in dc at end of previous row. Turn, (ch 4, 1 sc in next loop) twice, ch 2, 1 dc over 2-ch, 3 dc in dc, and 1 dc over next 2-ch, working these 5 dc into a Popcorn, ch 2, 1 sc in next loop, (ch 4, 1 sc in next) twice. Ch 6, turn, 1 sc in last loop, ch 4, 1 sc in next, ch 4, 1 sc in next 2-ch close to Popcorn, 1 sc in next 2-ch, (ch 4, 1 sc in next loop) twice, ch 2, 1 dc in at end of previous row. Turn, (ch 4, 1 sc in next loop) twice, ch 3, 1 sc in next, (ch 4, 1 sc in next) twice. Ch 6, turn, 1 sc in last loop, ch 4, 1 sc in next, ch 2, 5 dc over next 3-ch, remove hook, put hook through 1st dc from back to front, catch loop and pull through, forming a Popcorn in reverse, with the puff on the same side of work as previous Popcorns, ch 2, 1 sc in next loop, ch 4, 1 sc in next, ch 2, 1 dc in dc at end of previous row. Turn, ch 4, 1 sc in next loop, ch 4, 1 sc in 2-ch close to Popcorn, sk Popcorn, 1 sc in next 2-ch, *(ch 4, 1 sc in next*

Continued on page 57

Cotillion

MATERIALS:

J. & P. COATS KNIT-CRO-SHEEN

SINGLE SIZE
40 balls of White or Ecru,
or 64 balls of any color.

DOUBLE SIZE
48 balls of White or Ecru,
or 77 balls of any color.

OR

CLARK'S O.N.T. MERCERIZED BEDSPREAD COTTON

SINGLE SIZE
40 balls of White or Ecru.

DOUBLE SIZE
48 balls of White or Ecru.

Steel crochet hook No. 7 or 8.

GAUGE: Each block measures about 5½ inches square and 7¾ inches diagonally before blocking. For single size spread about 70 x 103 inches, make 213 motifs. For double size spread about 86 x 103 inches, make 263 motifs.

Cotillion

FIRST BLOCK . . . Ch 6, join with sl st to form ring. **1st rnd:** Ch 3, 15 dc in ring. Join with sl st in top st of 1st ch-3. **2nd rnd:** Ch 6 (to count as dc and ch-3), dc in same place as sl st, * ch 2, skip next dc, in next dc make dc, ch 3 and dc. Repeat from * around, joining last ch-2 to 3rd st of 1st ch-6. **3rd rnd:** Ch 3 (to count as dc), 4 dc in next ch-3 sp, drop loop from hook, insert hook in top of 1st ch-3 and pull dropped loop through (starting pc st made); * ch 2, dc in next ch-2 sp, ch 2, 5 dc in next ch-3 sp, drop loop from hook, insert hook in top of 1st dc of this group and pull dropped loop through (pc st made). Repeat from * around, joining last ch-2 to top of 1st pc st. **4th rnd:** Sl st in next sp, ch 3, a starting pc st in same sp, * ch 2, dc in next dc, (ch 2, pc st in next sp) twice. Repeat from * around. Join. **5th rnd:** Sl st in next sp, ch 3, a starting pc st in same sp, * ch 2, dc in next dc, (ch 2, pc st in next sp) 3 times. Repeat from * around. Join. **6th rnd:** Sl st in next sp, ch 3, a starting pc st in same sp, * ch 2, dc in next dc, (ch 2, pc st in next sp) 4 times. Repeat from * around. Join.

7th rnd: Sl st across to next dc, ch 3, 2 dc in same dc, * ch 5, skip 1 sp, (pc st in next sp, ch 2) twice; pc st in next dc, ch 5, sc in next dc, ch 5, skip 1 sp, (pc st in next sp, ch 2) twice; pc st in next sp, ch 5, 3 dc in next dc. Repeat from * around. Join. **8th rnd:** Ch 3, dc in same place as sl st, * in next dc make tr, ch 5 and tr, 2 dc in next dc, ch 6, pc st in next ch-2 sp, ch 2, pc st in next sp, (ch 6, sc in next loop) twice; ch 6, pc st in next sp, ch 2, pc st in next sp, ch 6, 2 dc in next dc. Repeat from * around. Join. **9th rnd:** Sl st to next sp, ch 3, in same sp make dc, tr, ch 5, tr and 2 dc; * ch 6, sc in next loop, ch 6, pc st in next sp, (ch 6, sc in next loop) 3 times; ch 6, pc st in next sp, ch 6, sc in next loop, ch 6, in next sp make 2 dc, tr, ch 5, tr and 2 dc. Repeat from * around. Join. **10th rnd:** Sl st to next sp, ch 3, in same sp make dc, tr, ch 7, tr and 2 dc, * (ch 6, sc in next loop) 8 times; ch 6, in next sp make 2 dc, tr, ch 7, tr and 2 dc. Repeat from * around. Join and fasten off.

SECOND BLOCK . . . Work as for 1st block to 9th rnd incl. **10th rnd:** Sl st to next sp, ch 3, in same sp make dc and tr; ch 3, sl st in corner sp of 1st block, ch 3, in same sp on 2nd block make tr and 2 dc; (ch 3, sl st in next loop on 1st block, ch 3, sc in next loop on 2nd block) 8 times; ch 3, sl st in next loop on 1st block, ch 3, in corner sp on 2nd block make 2 dc and tr; ch 3, sl st in corner sp of 1st block, ch 3, in same sp on 2nd block make tr and dc. Complete rnd as for 1st motif (no more joinings). Fasten off. Join all motifs in the same way (where 4 corners meet, join 3rd and 4th corners to joining of previous corners).

For single size spread make 213 blocks in all, joining them as follows: **1st row:** 1 block. **2nd row:** 3 blocks (one block extending on each side of 1st row). **3rd row:** 5 blocks. **4th row:** 7 blocks. Continue in this manner having 2 more blocks on each row until there are 17 blocks on row. Make 4 more rows of 17 blocks each, having 1 block extend beyond left edge and having 1 block less on right edge. Now make 2 blocks less on each row (1 block less on each side) until last row has one motif.

For double size spread make 263 motifs. Join as for single size spread until there are 21 blocks on row. Make 2 more rows of 21 blocks and continue as for single size spread.

EDGING . . . Attach thread in corner sp (following a joining) of single corner block. Ch 1, sc in same sp, * ch 2, in center st of same corner sp make 3 tr, ch 5 and 3 tr; ch 2, sc in same sp, (in center st of next loop make 3 tr, ch 5 and 3 tr, sc in next loop) 5 times. Repeat from * once more. Ch 5, sc in next corner sp. Continue thus around. Join and fasten off.

TASSELS . . . Cut a cardboard 5 inches wide and 4 inches long. Lay two 8-inch strands of thread across the length of cardboard. Wind thread 65 times around width of cardboard over the 8-inch strands. Slip off cardboard and tie ends of 8-inch strands. Cut loops at bottom of tassel. Wind thread several times around about ½ inch from top and fasten securely. Make 32 tassels for single size and 34 tassels for double size and sew to edge as in illustration along one narrow and two long edges.

Star and Flower Bedspread

Continued from page 55

loop) twice. Ch 6, turn, 1 sc in last loop, ch 4, 1 sc in next, ch 3, 1 sc in next, ch 4, 1 sc in next, ch 2, 1 dc in dc at end of previous row. Ch 4, turn, 1 sc in last 4-ch loop, ch 3, a Popcorn over next 3-ch, ch 3, 1 sc in next loop, ch 4, 1 sc in next. Ch 6, turn, 1 sc in next loop, ch 4, 1 sc in next 3-ch close to Popcorn, sk Popcorn, 1 sc in next 3-ch, ch 4, 1 sc in next loop, ch 2, 1 dc in dc at end of previous row. Ch 4, turn, 1 sc in last 4-ch loop, ch 2, 1 sc in next, ch 4, 1 sc in next. Ch 6, turn, 1 sc in last loop, ch 2, a Popcorn over next 2-ch, worked in reverse, so the puff is on same side of work as the rest, ch 2, 1 sc in next loop, ch 2, 1 dc in dc at end of previous row. Ch 4, turn, 1 sc in 2-ch close to Popcorn, sk Popcorn, 1 sc in next 2-ch, ch 4, 1 sc in next loop. Ch 6, turn, 1 sc in last loop, ch 1, 1 sc in next, ch 2, 1 dc in dc at end of previous row. Ch 3, turn, sk 1 ch in center of last row, 1 sc in next loop. Ch 3, turn, 1 dc in 3-ch, ch 3, 1 sl st in dc at end of previous row. Fasten off, leaving a 2-inch thread hanging. Sk next 8 spaces down side of Point, join again to next space, ch 1, turn, (3 sc over next space) 9 times,

working over 2-inch thread left from Point, 3 sc in back loop of next dc, (3 sc over next space) 9 times, 1 sc in next dc. Fasten off, leaving a 10-inch thread hanging, to use in sewing Points together. Make 2 Lattice Points for Star Block. Sew the bases of the 4 Points together, completing Block. Make 154 Star Blocks.

On tissue paper, draw a true circle slightly larger than finished Flower Blocks. Stretch and pin each Flower right-side-down on such a pattern and steam with a wet cloth and hot iron, then press through a dry cloth until perfectly dry. Press the Star Blocks in same way. A Spread pressed in this way will keep its shape and flatness indefinitely. Sew Blocks together, following illustration.

To fill in spaces between Flowers around outside of Spread, make 50 separate Star Points, both Solid and Lattice, and sew them in place alternately.

TASSELS—Wind thread 36 times around a 3-inch cardboard, tie at one end and cut at other end. Wind a thread ½-inch from top and tie. Sew tassels in places as shown in illustration around sides and bottom of Spread.

Land of Nod

Whimsical . . . elfin . . . and so simple to make, a block of filet crochet and then a block of fabric. Little tots will adore it.

Materials Required—
AMERICAN THREAD COMPANY
"STAR" MERCERIZED CROCHET COTTON

15 250-yd. Balls White, Size 20.
2½ yds. Linen.
Steel Crochet Hook No. 10.

Each Motif measures about 7½ inches. Finished Linen square measures about 7½ inches. 14 Crocheted motifs and 14 Linen squares are required for cover illustrated. If a larger cover is desired add more motifs for length and width.

FILET MOTIF. Ch 107, d c in 8th st from hook, * ch 2, skip 2 sts, d c in next st, repeat from * across row, (34 meshes) ch 5, turn.

2nd Row—D c in d c, * ch 2, d c in next d c, repeat from * across row and continue working back and forth according to diagram working 4 d c for each solid mesh and 3 d c for each additional solid mesh.

Work one of each design and around each motif work a row of s c working 2 s c over each mesh and 5 s c over each mesh at corner, break thread.

Cut a square of linen same size as crocheted motif allowing ⅜ inch on all sides for a very narrow hem. Work a row of s c over hem, break thread.

Sew crocheted motifs and linen squares together as illustrated.

SIDE TUCK IN. Cut a piece of material same length as cover and 11 inches wide allowing ⅜ inch for a very narrow hem. Work a row of s c all around, ch 3, turn, 2 d c in same space, skip 2 s c, sl st in next s c, * ch 3, 2 d c in same space, skip 2 s c, sl st in next s c, repeat from * on 2 short and 1 long side.

Sew to cover with Star Twist Mercerized Sewing Thread. Finish other side and lower edge in same manner.

Double Bed Size, approximately:
82 inches by 101 inches.

MATERIALS—
Bucilla Petite Wondersheen (mercerized) Cotton,
Article 3799, 19 skeins,
or
Bucilla Wondersheen (mercerized) Cotton,
Article 3666, 19 skeins,
or

Bucilla Blue Label (delustered) Cotton,
Article 3457, 17 skeins.
FOR THE PETITE WONDERSHEEN USE—
1 Bucilla Steel Crochet Hook, Size 8, Article 4300.
FOR THE WONDERSHEEN AND BLUE LABEL USE—
1 Bucilla Steel Crochet Hook, Size 9, Article 4300.
Gauge: Each square should measure 5 inches.

Cross-bar Popcorn Bedspread

SQUARE MOTIF—Ch 8, work 1 d c in first st of chain, ch 5, 1 d c in same st, ch 5 and 1 more d c in same st, ch 3, join with a d c in 3rd st of chain 8 at beginning of round. **2nd round:** ch 3, work 5 d c around the post of joining d c below, 1 d c in same place as the joining d c, * 11 d c in next space, 1 d c in top of next d c; repeat from * twice, then work 5 d c in next space, join with a slip st in top st of chain 3 at beginning of round. **3rd round:** ch 5, * skip 2 sts, work 1 d c in each of the next 7 sts, ch 2, skip 2 sts, work a group of 1 d c, ch 5, 1 d c, —all in next st (corner), ch 2; repeat from * around, end with ch 2 after the group of 7 d c, 1 d c in joining st of round below, ch 3, join with a d c in 3rd st of chain 5 at beginning of round. **4th round:** ch 5, work 1 d c in same place as the joining d c of round below was worked in, * ch 2, skip the next space, work 1 d c in top of each of the next 7 d c below, ch 2 and 1 d c in top of next d c, ch 2, work 1 d c in center st of corner chain, ch 2, work 5 d c in same st; drop loop from hook, insert it in the top of first d c of group of 5 just made, insert it also in the dropped loop and draw through (a popcorn), ch 2, 1 d c in same place, ch 2, 1 d c in top of next d c; repeat from * around, end with ch 2, 1 d c in top of joining d c below, ch 2, work a popcorn in same st, join with a d c in 3rd st of chain 5 at beginning of round. **5th round:** ch 5, work 1 d c in same place as the joining d c, * ch 2 and 1 d c in top of each of the next 2 d c, ch 2, skip 2 sts, work 1 d c in top of next d c, ch 2, skip the next 2 sts, 1 d c in top of next d c, ch 2 and 1 d c in top of each of the next 2 d c, ch 2, work a group of 1 d c, ch 2, a popcorn, ch 2, 1 d c, —all in top of corner popcorn, ch 2 and 1 d c in top of next d c; repeat from * around, end same as in last round. **6th round:** ch 5, work 1 d c in same place as the joining d c below, ch 2 and 1 d c in top of each d c to next corner, work a group of ch 2, 1 d c, ch 2, a popcorn, ch 2, 1 d c, —all in top of popcorn below, ch 2 and 1 d c in top of each d c to next corner, work this corner same as last, then continue in same way around, being careful to have all corners alike, end and join as before. Repeat last round twice. **9th round:** ch 5, work 1 d c in same place as the joining d c below, ch 2 and 1 d c in top of each d c to next corner, work a group of ch 2, 1 d c, ch 5, 1 d c, —all in top of corner popcorn below, ch 2 and 1 d c in top of each d c to next corner, work this corner like last, then continue around, working all corners alike, end with ch 2 and 1 d c in top of last popcorn of round, ch 3, join with a d c in 3rd st of chain 5 at beginning of round. **Final round:** ch 5, thread twice over hook, draw up a loop in top of joining d c below, over and through 2 loops, twice in succession; retaining the last 2 loops on hook, thread twice over hook, draw up a loop in same place, over and through 2 loops, twice in succession, over and through the remaining 3 loops on hook (a treble petal at beginning of round), ch 3, thread over hook, draw up a loop in same place, over and through 2 loops on hook; retaining the last 2 loops on hook, thread over, draw up another loop in same place, over and through 2; retaining the 3 loops now on hook, thread over and draw up a 3rd loop in same place, over and through 2 loops, over and through remaining 4 loops on hook (a d c petal), † * ch 5, skip 2 spaces, work a d c petal in top of next d c; repeat from * 7 times, ch 5, skip next space, work a d c petal in center st of next corner space, ch 3, work a regular treble petal in same st as follows: thread twice over hook, draw up a loop in st, over and through 2 loops, twice in succession; retaining the last 2 loops on hook, thread twice over hook, draw up a 2nd loop in same place, thread over and through 2 loops twice in succession; retaining the 3 loops now on hook, thread twice over hook and draw up a 3rd loop in same place, over and through 2 loops, twice in succession, over and through remaining 4 loops on hook, ch 3, work a d c petal in same st; repeat from † around, end with ch 5 and a d c petal in same place as the first 2 petals of round, ch 3, join with a slip st in top of first treble petal and fasten off thread. This completes one square, make 266 of these squares.

Arrange squares, 14 in width and 19 in length; sew from wrong side with an overhand stitch, taking up top thread from each edge st and being careful to have seams as elastic as the crocheted fabric. Darn in all ends neatly.

FRINGE—Wind thread around a 6½ inch cardboard and cut at one end. Tie an 8-strand fringe in each space along 3 sides of spread (2 long sides and 1 short side), as shown in illustration. Trim fringe evenly to 6 inches and darn in all ends neatly.

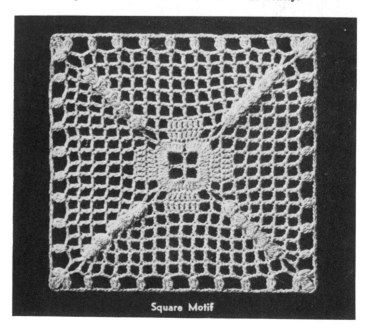

Square Motif

Lotus Flower Bedspread

Double Bed Size, approximately: 85 inches by 102 inches.

MATERIALS—
Bucilla Petite Wondersheen (mercerized) Cotton, Article 3799, 31 skeins,
or
Bucilla Wondersheen (mercerized) Cotton, Article 3666, 31 skeins,
or
Bucilla Blue Label (delustered) Cotton, Article 3457, 27 skeins.

FOR THE PETITE WONDERSHEEN USE—
1 Bucilla Steel Crochet Hook, Size 7, Article 4300.

FOR THE WONDERSHEEN AND BLUE LABEL USE—
1 Bucilla Steel Crochet Hook, Size 8, Article 4300.

Gauge: Each square should measure 7½ inches.

SQUARE MOTIF—Ch 8, join with a slip st into a ring. **1st round:** work 16 s c in ring; join with a slip st in first s c of round. **2nd round:** ch 3, work 4 d c in joining st of round below, drop loop from hook, insert it in top st of chain 3, insert it also in the dropped loop and draw through (a popcorn at beginning of round), * ch 2, skip next st, 5 d c in next st; drop loop from hook, insert it in top of first d c of the group of 5 d c just made, insert it also in the dropped loop and draw through (popcorn); repeat from * around, end with ch 2, join with a slip st in top of popcorn at beginning of round. **3rd round:** ch 5, 1 d c in space after first popcorn, * ch 2, 1 d c in top of next popcorn, ch 2 and 1 d c in next space; repeat from * around, end with ch 2, join with a slip st in 3rd st of chain 5 at beginning of round. **4th round:** ch 1, work 1 s c in joining st below, * 3 s c in next space, 1 s c in top of next d c; repeat from * around, end with 3 s c in last space, join with a slip st in first s c of round. **5th round:** ch 1, work 2 s c on back thread of joining st in round below, * 1 s c on back thread of each of the next 3 sts, 3 s c on back thread of next st; repeat from * around, end with 1 s c in same place as the first 2 s c of round, join with a slip st in first s c of round. Always work on back thread of all sts unless otherwise mentioned. **6th round:** ch 1, work 2 s c in joining st, * 1 s c in each of the next 5 sts, 3 s c in next st; repeat from * around, end with 1 s c in same place as the first 2 s c of round, join with a slip st in first s c. Continue to work in this way, increasing (3 s c in 1 st) at center of each of the 16 points, until there are 10 rounds completed from beginning, when there will be 15 sts between center sts at points. **11th round:** slip st in each of the next 5 sts, then fold and join pleats as follows: place next point on top of first point (folding right side of work inside), work 1 s c in next st, inserting hook under top thread of both sts, join the next 2 edge sts in same way, * ch 3, fold the next 2 points together as before, skip 5 sts from point and join the next 3 sts of both edges in same way; repeat from * around until all "petals" are joined; end with ch 3 and join with a slip st in the first of the 3 joining s c of first petal. **12th round:** ch 1, work 1 s c on back thread of joining st below, 1 s c on back thread of each st to end of round, join with a slip st in first

s c of round. **13th round:** ch 8, work a long treble (3 times over hook) in joining st, taking up both threads of st, ch 1, 1 more long treble in same st, take up both threads of sts in this round, * ch 1, skip 1 st, 1 treble (twice over hook) in next st, ch 1, skip 1 st, 1 d c in next st, ch 1, skip 1 st, work 1 s d c (s d c—short d c—thread over hook, draw up a loop in st, over and through all 3 loops on hook) in next st, ch 1, skip 1 st, 1 s c in each of the next 9 sts, ch 1, skip 1 st, 1 s d c in next st, ch 1, skip 1 st, 1 d c in next st, ch 1, skip 1 st, 1 treble in next st, ch 1, skip 1 st, work a long treble in next st, ch 1, a 2nd long treble in same st, ch 1 and a 3rd long treble in same st, ch 1 and a 4th long treble in same st, ch 1 and a 5th long treble in same st (corner); repeat from * around, end with ch 1 and a long treble in same place as the first group of long trebles at beginning of round, ch 1 and a 2nd long treble in same place, ch 1, join with a slip st in 7th st of chain 8 at beginning of round. **14th round:** ch 1, turn, working on front thread of all stitches in this round, work 2 s c in joining st below, 1 s c in each st to next corner, 3 s c in corner st, 1 s c in each st to next corner, work this corner like last, then continue around, working all corners alike, end with 1 s c in same place the group of 2 s c at beginning of round was worked in, join with a slip st in first s c. **15th round:** ch 6, turn, work 1 treble in joining st below (take up both threads of all stitches in this round), ch 1 and 1 more treble in same st, † * ch 1, skip 1 st, 1 treble in next st; repeat from * 15 times, ch 1, skip next st, work 1 treble in next st (corner), ch 1 and a 2nd treble in same st, ch 1 and a 3rd treble in same st, ch 1 and a 4th treble in same st, ch 1 and a 5th treble in same st; repeat from † around, end with ch 1, a treble in same place as the first group of trebles in round, ch 1 and 1 more treble in same place, ch 1, join with a slip st in 5th

Continued on page 65

Square Motif

Fairy Ring Bedspread

MATERIALS—Lily's Skytone Mercerized Crochet Cotton in White, Cream, Ecru, Beige or Ivory. Single Size—39 balls. Double Size—46 balls. Steel Crochet Hook Size 8 or 9.

GAUGE—Each block measures about 6¼ inches square when blocked and requires 76 yds. For a single size spread about 75x106 inches, make 12x17 blocks. For a double size spread about 87½x106 inches, make 14x17 blocks.

BLOCK—Ch 4 for a dc, * ch 4, 3 dc in 4th st from hook, ch 2, sl st in same st, ch 5, 3 dc in 4th st from hook, ch 2, sl st in same st, 1 dc in starting st of work. Repeat from * 3 times, joining last shell with a sl st in top of 1st 4-ch.

Row 2—Ch 3, remove hook, insert in center-top of next shell, catch loop and pull thru, letting ch lie up back of shell, * ch 6, (1 dc, 3tr and 1 dc) in 4th st from hook, ch 2, sl st in same st, ch 2, 1 sc in next shell. Repeat from * 7 times.

Row 3—Sl st in next 2-ch, ch 4, run up back of next shell and catch at center-top (as before) * ch 5, sc in 4th st from hook for a p, ch 7, (1 dc, 7 tr and 1 dc) in 4th st from hook, ch 2, sl st in same st, ch 6, p, ch 2, sc in next shell. Repeat from * 7 times. Fasten off.

Row 4—Join to 1st tr on last shell, ch 1, 1 hdc in same st, * 3 dc in next, 1 hdc and 1 sc in next tr, ch 3, (4 tr, ch 5, sl st in last tr for a p, and 4 tr) in back loop of next tr, ch 3, 1 sc and 1 hdc in next tr, 3 dc in next, 1 hdc and 1 sc in next tr, ch 21, sl st in 3d st of long ch, counting from last sc, ch 2, 1 sc and 1 hdc in 1st tr on next shell. Repeat from * around. Fasten off.

Row 5—Join to last long loop, * ch 10, 1 sc in p at tip of next shell, ch 8, 1 dtr in next long loop, (ch 3, 1 dtr, ch 7, 1 dtr, ch 3 and 1 dtr) in same loop, ch 8, 1 sc in next p, ch 10, 1 sc in next long loop. Repeat from * around.

Row 6—Ch 3 and work dc around, putting 10 dc over each 10-ch, 8 dc over each 8-ch, 3 dc over each 3-ch, and 1 dc in each sc and dtr. In corner 7-chs, make 3 dc, 5 dc in 4th st, and 3 dc in bal. Join to starting 3-ch.

Row 7—Ch 3, 1 dc in same st, * ch 2, 2 dc in next 3d dc, holding the last loop of each dc on hook, thread over and pull thru all 3 loops at once (a Cluster). Repeat from * to next corner st. Ch 5, a 2-dc-Cluster in same corner st. Repeat From * around. Join final 2-ch to 1st dc.

Row 8—(3 sc in next 2-ch space) 4 times, * ch 3, turn, skip 2 sc, (1 dc, ch 4 and 1 dc) in next sc, ch 3, sl st in next 3d sc, ch 1, turn, 4 sc over each 3-ch, 5 sc over 4-ch. 2 sc in next beading space, (3 sc in next) twice. Repeat from * to corner. 6 sc in corner space, ch 3, turn, skip 2 sc, (1 dc, ch 3, 1 tr, ch 4, 1 tr, ch 3, and 1 dc) in next sc, ch 3, sl st in next 2d sc, ch 1, turn, 4 sc over each 3-ch, 5 sc over 4-ch. 1 sc in same corner space, (3 sc in next 2-ch) twice. Repeat from * around. Sl st in 1st 3 sc and make a final scallop. Fasten off.

Make the necessary number of blocks and tack together with neat over-and-over stitches on wrong side. Join by the tips of the 7 scallops across each side and by the 2d and 4th sc on center space of each corner scallop. Block to measurements given.

Lotus Flower Bedspread
Continued from page 62

st of chain 6 at beginning of round. **16th round:** ch 1, turn, work on front thread of all sts in this round, work 3 s c in joining st, 1 s c in each st to next corner, 4 s c in corner st, 1 s c in each st to next corner, work this corner same as last, then continue in this way around, working all corners alike, end with 1 s c in same place as the first 3 s c of round, join with a slip st in first s c. **17th round:** ch 3, turn, work a popcorn in joining st of round below (as described for popcorn at beginning of round), take up both threads of every st in this round, ch 2, work a regular popcorn in same st, † * ch 2, skip 2 sts, work a popcorn in next st; repeat from * 13 times, ch 2, skip 2 sts, a popcorn in next (corner) st, ch 2 and a 2nd popcorn in same st, ch 2 and a 3rd popcorn in same st; repeat from † around, end with ch 2 and a popcorn in same place as the first 2 popcorns of round, ch 2, join with a slip st in top of first popcorn. **18th round:** ch 1, turn, work 2 s c in top of corner popcorn, 3 s c in each space to next corner, work 3 s c in top of corner popcorn, then 3 s c in each space to next corner, work this corner like last, continue in same way around, working all corners alike, end with 1 s c in same place as the 2 s c at beginning of round, join with a slip st in first s c. **19th round:** ch 6, turn, working on both threads of all sts in this round, work 1 treble in joining st below, ch 1 and another treble in same st, † * ch 1, skip 1 st, 1 treble in next st; repeat from * to next corner, work ch 1 and 1 treble in corner st, ch 1 and a 2nd treble in same st, ch 1 and a 3rd treble in same st, ch 1 and a 4th treble in same st, ch 1 and a 5th treble in same st; then repeat from † around, end with ch 1, work 1 treble in same place as the trebles at beginning of round, ch 1 and 1 more treble in same place, ch 1, join with a slip st in 5th st of chain 6 at beginning of round. **20th round:** ch 1, turn, work all sts of this round on front thread of stitches, work 3 s c in joining st below, * 1 s c in each st to next corner, work 5 s c

in corner st; repeat from * around, working all corners alike, end with 2 s c in same place as the 3 s c at beginning of round, join with a slip st in first s c of round. **21st round:** ch 3, turn, taking up both threads of sts in this round, work a popcorn (as at beginning of round) in joining st below, ch 2, a regular popcorn in same place, † * ch 2, skip 2 sts, a popcorn in next st; repeat from * to next corner, work a group of ch 2, 1 popcorn, ch 2, a popcorn, ch 2 and another popcorn, —all in corner st; repeat from † around, end with ch 2, a popcorn in same place as the 2 popcorns at beginning of round, ch 2, join with a slip st in top of first popcorn. **22nd round:** ch 1, turn, work 3 s c in joining st below, * 3 s c in each space to next corner, 4 s c in top of corner popcorn; repeat from * around, end with 1 s c in same place as the first 3 s c of round and join with a slip st in first s c. **23rd round:** ch 6, turn, working on both threads of all sts in this round, work 1 treble in joining st below, ch 1 and a 2nd treble in same st, † * ch 1, skip 1 st, work a treble in next st; repeat from * 37 times, ch 1 and a 2nd treble in same st, ch 1 and 3rd treble in same st, ch 1 and a 4th treble in same st, ch 1 and a 5th treble in same st, then repeat from † around, end with ch 1, 1 treble in same place as the corner group at beginning of round, ch 1 and another treble in same place, ch 1, join with a slip st in 5th st of chain 6 at beginning of round and fasten off thread. This completes one square, make 130 of these squares.

Arrange squares 10 squares in width and 13 squares in length; sew from wrong side with an overhand stitch, taking up top thread of each edge st and being careful to keep seams as elastic as the crocheted fabric.

FRINGE—Wind thread around a 6-inch cardboard and cut at one end, tie a 4-strand fringe in every other space of round on 3 sides of spread (2 long sides and lower edge). Divide fringes in half and tie another knot about 1 inch below first knot, taking 4 strands from first fringe and 4 strands from third fringe (as shown in illustration). Trim fringe evenly to 5 inches and darn in all ends neatly.

Sunflower Bedspread

Approximate Size: 85 inches by 102 inches.

MATERIALS: Bucilla Wondersheen Perlé, Article 3783, 40 skeins.

1 Bucilla Aluminum 6-inch Crochet Hook, Size 4, Article 3853.

or

1 Bucilla White 6-inch Crochet Hook, Size 4, Article 3840.

Gauge: Each octagon should measure 8½ inches in diameter.

OCTAGON—Ch 3, join with a slip st into a ring, work 8 s c in ring, then work 2 s c in each st of round below, join with a slip st in first s c of round (16 s c in round). Petal round: ch 1, work 1 s c in joining st, * ch 12, 1 s c in 2nd st from hook, 1 s d c (short d c—thread over hook, draw up a loop in st, over and through all 3 loops on hook) in next st, 1 d c in each of the next 7 sts, 1 s d c in next st, 1 s c in last st of chain, 1 s c in next st of round below, 1 s c in next st; repeat from * around, end with 1 s c in last st, after 8th petal, join with a slip st in first s c of round and fasten off thread. 1st round: make a loop on hook and working from right side, beginning in tip of any petal, work 1 s c in first s c made on petal, 1 s c in top of each of the next 6 sts on side of petal, * ch 1, skip 4 sts on foundation chain of next petal, 1 s c in each of the next 7 sts (along foundation chain of petal to tip), ch 1, 1 s c in each of the next 7 sts on petal (along other side of petal); repeat from * around, end with ch 1, a s c in each of the 7 sts on foundation chain of first petal, ch 1, join with a slip st in first s c of round. 2nd round: ch 6, work 1 d c under the ch 1 just made, * ch 5, skip 3 sts, thread twice over hook, draw up a loop in next st, over and through 2 loops twice in succession, thread twice over hook, draw up a loop in center s c on first side of next petal, over and through 2, twice in succession, over and through remaining 3 loops on hook (a decreasing treble), ch 5, 1 d c under ch 1 on tip of same petal, ch 3, 1 more d c in same place; repeat from * around, end with ch 5, join with a slip st in 3rd st of ch 6 at beginning of round, slip st in next st. 3rd round: 1 s c in next st, † ch 1, 1 s c in same st, * ch 1, skip 1 st, 1 s c on back thread of next st; repeat from * 7 times, then repeat from † around, end with ch 1, join with a slip st in first s c of round, slip st in next st. 4th round: ch 6, 1 d c in same st as last slip st, * ch 2, skip 2 sts, 1 d c on back thread of next s c, ch 2, skip 2 sts, 1 d c in next chain st, ch 2, skip 2 sts, 1 d c on back thread of next s c, ch 3, slip st in top of the d c just made (picot), ch 2, skip 2 sts, 1 d c in next chain st, ch 2, skip 2 sts, 1 d c on back thread of next s c, ch 2, skip 2 sts, 1 d c in corner chain st, ch 3, 1 d c in same place, ch 2, skip 2 sts, 1 d c on back thread of next s c, ch 3, picot, ch 2, skip 2 sts, 1 d c in next chain st, ch 2, skip 2 sts, 1 d c on back thread of next s c, ch 5, picot, ch 2, skip 2 sts, 1 d c in next chain st, ch 2, skip 2 sts, 1 d c on back thread of next s c, ch 3, picot, ch 2, skip 2 sts, 1 d c in next corner chain st, ch 3, 1 more d c in same st; repeat from * around, thus working 1 picot on one side and 3 picots on the next side in alternate fashion, end with ch 2, join with a slip st in 3rd st of chain 6 at beginning of round and fasten off thread. This completes one octagon, make 120 of these motifs.

SQUARE—Ch 5, join with a slip st into a ring, 1 s c in ring, * ch 5, thread twice over hook, draw up a loop in ring, over and through 2 loops twice in succession, retaining the last 2 loops on hook, thread twice over hook, draw up another loop in same ring, over and through 2 loops, 3 times in succession, over and through remaining 2 loops on hook, ch 5, 1 s c in ring; repeat from * 3 times, but the last time omit the s c after the ch 5 and join with a slip st in first s c of round; fasten off thread. 2nd round: make a loop on hook and work 1 d c in top st of any petal in round below, * ch 3, 1 more d c in same place, ch 5, thread twice over hook, draw up a loop in center st of next ch 5, thread over and through 2 loops twice in succession, thread twice over hook, draw up a loop in center st of next ch 5, over and through 2 loops twice in succession, over and through the remaining 3 loops on hook (a decreasing treble), ch 5, 1 d c in top of next petal; repeat from * around, end with ch 5, join with a slip st in top of first d c of round, slip st in each of the next 2 sts. 3rd round: * ch 5, slip st in same st, slip st on back thread of each of the next 8 sts, ch 3, slip st in same st, slip st on back thread of each of the next 8 sts; repeat from * around, join with a slip st in first st and fasten off thread. This completes one square, make 99 of these squares. Arrange motifs in places as shown on diagram on and tack with a strong tacking.

EDGING—Working from right side make a loop on hook and work 1 s c in any space of round, * ch 5, slip st in 3rd st from hook, ch 2, 1 s c in next space; repeat from * around entire spread, join with a slip st in first s c of round and fasten off thread. Darn in all ends neatly.

BEDSPREAD

Flower Queen

A raised flower motif gives the illusion of a lovely nosegay

Materials Required: AMERICAN THREAD COMPANY "DE LUXE" CROCHET AND KNITTING COTTON, ARTICLE 346 OR "PURITAN" BEDSPREAD COTTON, ARTICLE 40
89—250 yd. Balls Cream, Ecru or White.
Each Motif measures about 5 inches. 286 Motifs 13 x 22 are required for Bedspread measuring about 65 x 110 inches without the Border.
Steel Crochet Hook No. 7.

MOTIF: Ch 8, join to form a ring, ch 3, * thread over hook, insert in ring, pull loop through, repeat from * once, thread over and work off all loops but one, thread over and work off 2 loops, ch 3, * thread over hook, insert in ring, pull loop through, repeat from * twice, thread over and work off all loops but one, thread over, work off 2 loops (puff st), ch 3 and work 6 more puff sts with ch 3 between each puff st in ring, ch 3, join in 1st puff st.

2nd Row. Sl st to next loop, ch 3, d c in same space, * ch 5, 2 d c in next loop, repeat from * 6 times, ch 5, join.

3rd Row. Sl st to loop, ch 3 and work 3 puff sts with ch 2 between each puff st in same loop, * ch 2, 3 puff sts with ch 2 between each puff st in next loop, repeat from * all around, ch 2, join in 1st puff st.

4th Row. Sl st to the center puff st, * ch 9, s c in top of center puff st of next group, repeat from * 7 times.

5th Row. Sl st into loop, ch 3 (counts as 1 d c), work 24 d c over loop, * ch 2, work 25 d c in next loop, repeat from * 6 times, ch 2, join.

6th Row. Ch 4, d c in next d c, * ch 1, d c in next d c, repeat from * 19 times, ch 1, sl loop off hook, bring petal forward, insert hook into 3rd d c of same petal, pull loop through, ch 1, d c in next d c, * ch 1, d c in next d c, repeat from * once, ch 2 and start 2nd petal, work 9 d c with ch 1 between each d c, ch 1, sl loop from hook, insert hook in corresponding d c of previous petal and pull loop through, thus joining petals, ch 1, work 13 d c with ch 1 between each d c, ch 1, sl loop off hook, bring petal forward, insert hook into 4th d c of petal being made, pull loop through, ch 1 and work 1 d c with ch 1 between in each remaining d c of petal, ch 2 and work 5 more petals in same manner. Last petal, work 9 d c with ch 1 between each d c, ch 1 and join to previous petal, ch 1, work 8 d c with ch 1 between each d c, ch 1, join to corresponding d c of 1st petal, ch 1, work 5 d c with ch 1 between each d c, ch 1, join to 4th d c of petal being made, ch 1, complete petal, ch 2, join row.

7th Row. Ch 1 and work 2 s c in each ch 1 loop and 4 s c in each ch 2 loop (16 s c in each section between petals), do not join.

8th Row. Sl st in each of the next 11 s c, * ch 6, skip 6 s c, work 1 s c in each of the next 10 sts, ch 3, skip 6 s c, 1 s c in each of the next 10 sts, repeat from * 3 times.

9th Row. Sl st in loop, ch 4, thread over hook, insert in same loop, work off 2 loops, thread over, insert in same loop and work off all loops 2 at a time, ch 3, * thread over hook, insert in same loop and work off 2 loops, repeat from * twice and work off remaining loops 2 at a time (cluster st), work 2 more cluster sts with ch 3 between in same space, * ch 3, work 1 s c in each of the 6 center s c of s c group, ch 3, d c in center ch of next loop, ch 2, d c in same space (shell), ch 3, 1 s c in each of the 6 center s c of next s c group, ch 3, 4 cluster sts with ch 3 between each cluster st in next ch 6 loop and repeat from * all around, ch 3, join in 1st cluster st.

10th Row. Sl st in ch 3 loop, ch 4, work 2 cluster sts with ch 2 between in same space, ch 2, cluster st in next space, ch 5, cluster st in same space, ch 2, 2 cluster sts with ch 2 between in next space, ch 5, 1 s c in each of the 4 center s c of s c group, ch 5, shell in shell, ch 5, 1 s c in each of the 4 center s c of next s c group, ch 5 and continue all around in same manner, ch 5, join in 1st cluster st.

11th Row. Sl st to loop, 3 s c in each of the next 2 loops, 7 s c in corner loop, 3 s c in each of the next 2 loops, 3 s c over ch 5 loop, ch 3, d c in 3rd s c, ch 3, 3 s c over end of next ch 5 loop, 3 s c in shell, work 2nd half of side to correspond and continue in same manner all around, join.

12th Row. Work 1 s c in each s c on sides, 3 s c in center s c at each corner and 3 s c over each ch 3, join (45 s c on each side and 3 s c in each corner).

13th Row. Sl st to corner, ch 3 and work a puff st in corner, ch 3, puff st in same space, ch 1, puff st in next st, * ch 1, skip 1 s c, puff st in next st, repeat from * 22 times, ch 1, 2 puff sts with ch 3 between in corner st and continue all around in same manner (24 puff sts on each side and 2 puff sts in each corner).

14th Row. Sl st to corner loop and work 2 s c, ch 3, 2 s c in corner and 2 s c in each ch 1 loop on sides, break thread. Work 285 more motifs in same manner. Sew motifs together having 13 motifs in width and 22 motifs in length.

BORDER: Attach thread in 1st s c to left of any corner, work a row of s c around spread, having an uneven number of s c on sides, and 3 s c in each corner, join in 1st s c.

2nd Row. Sl st to next s c, ch 3, * thread over hook, insert in same space, pull loop up the length of a d c, repeat from * once, thread over and pull through all loops but one on hook, thread over and pull through 2 loops, ** ch 1, skip 1 s c, thread over hook, insert in next st, pull loop up the length of a d c, * thread over hook, insert in same space, pull loop up same length, repeat from * once, thread over and pull through all loops but one, thread over and pull through 2 loops (puff st), repeat from ** to within 2 sts of center st at corner, ch 1, skip 1 s t, puff st in 1st s c of corner, ch 1, 2 puff sts with ch 3 between in center s c, ch 1, puff st in next s c, ch 1, work all sides and corners in same manner, ending row with ch 1, join in 1st puff st.

Continued on page 70

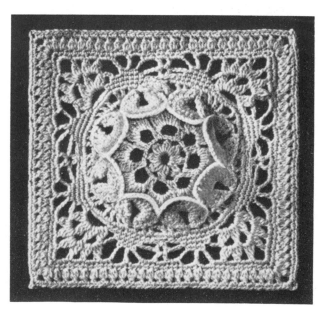

69

Arrow and Rose

Shown on page 49

STRIP . . . Starting at the bottom, ch 166 (to measure about 15 inches). **1st row:** Dc in 4th ch from hook and in next 5 ch, (ch 3, skip 2 ch, sc in next ch, ch 3, skip 2 ch, dc in next ch) twice; (ch 2, skip 2 ch, dc in next ch) 3 times; dc in next 6 ch, ch 2, skip 2 ch, dc in next ch (sp made), dc in next 6 ch. Make 15 sps, dc in next 3 ch (bl made), make 10 sps, dc in next 6 ch, 1 sp, dc in next 6 ch, 3 sps, ch 3, skip 2 ch, sc in next ch, ch 3, skip 2 ch, dc in next ch (lacet made). Make 1 more lacet, dc in next 6 ch. Ch 5, turn. **2nd row:** Skip 2 dc, dc in next dc, ch 2, skip 2 dc, dc in next dc (2 sps made over 2 bls), ch 5, dc in next dc (bar made over lacet). Make 1 more bar, ch 2, dc in next dc (sp made over sp), make 2 more sps,

dc in next 3 dc (bl made over bl). Make 1 sp, 2 dc in next sp, dc in next dc (bl made over sp). Make 13 sps, 1 bl, 16 sps, 1 bl, 1 sp, 1 bl, 3 sps, 2 bars, 2 sps. Ch 3, turn. **3rd row:** 2 bls, ch 3, skip 2 ch, sc in next ch, ch 3, dc in next dc (lacet made over bar). Make 3 sps, 2 bls, 1 sp, 4 bls, 13 sps, 1 bl, 12 sps, 4 bls, 1 sp, 2 bls, 3 sps, 1 lacet, 1 bl, then make 2 dc in next sp, dc in 3rd st of turning ch. Ch 5, turn. Starting with 4th row, follow chart to top. Repeat the 1st to 88th rows incl of chart 3 more times; then work the 1st to 78th rows once more. Fasten off.

Block strip to measure 13½ x 107 inches. Make the necessary number of strips and sew them together with neat over-and-over stitches on wrong side.

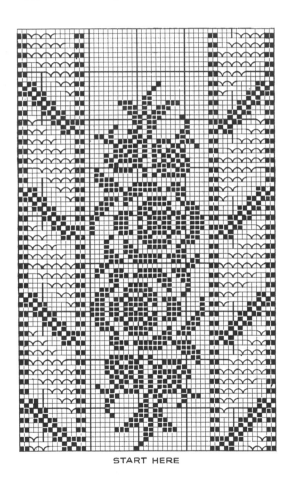

START HERE

There are 10 spaces between heavy lines

Flower Queen
Continued from page 69

3rd Row. Sl st into ch 1 loop, ch 3, puff st in same space, * ch 1, puff st in next ch 1 loop, repeat from * to the ch 1 loop before the corner ch 3 loop, ch 1, 2 puff sts with ch 1 between in next loop, ch 1, 2 puff sts with ch 3 between in corner loop, ch 1, 2 puff sts with ch 1 between in next loop, work all sides and corners in same manner, ending row with ch 1, join in 1st puff st.
4th Row. Sl st into loop, ch 3, puff st in same space, * ch 1,

puff st in next loop, repeat from * to the loop before the corner loop, ch 1, 2 puff sts with ch 1 between in next loop, ch 1, 2 puff sts with ch 1 between in corner loop, ch 3, 2 puff sts with ch 1 between in same loop, ch 1, 2 puff sts with ch 1 between in next loop, work all sides and corners in same manner, ending row with ch 1, join in 1st puff st. Repeat last row once.
Next Row. Sl st into next loop, work 2 s c in each ch 1 loop and 2 s c, ch 3, 2 s c in each corner loop, join.
Next Row. Work 1 s c in each s c and 5 s c in each corner loop, join, break thread.

DOILIES

Oriental Fantasy

MATERIALS—2-balls Sil-Tone Mercerized Crochet Cotton in White. Crochet hook size 9. Size—16".

(Ch 7, a 3-tr-Cluster in 7th st from hook, ch 4, sl st in Cluster for a p, ch 6, sl st at base of Cluster) 4 times, sl st in 1st st, ch 6, fasten up back of 1st petal with a sl st in 1st p. **ROW 2**—(Ch 13, sc in next petal) 4 times. **ROW 3**—Ch 1, (15 sc in next sp, 1 sc in sc) repeated around, sl st in 1st 1-ch. **ROW 4**—Ch 5, dc in 2 dc, sc, (ch 2, dc in next 2d sc) repeated around, sl st in 3d st of 5-ch. **ROW 5**—3 sc in each sp around. Sl st in 1st 2 sc. **ROW 6**—Ch 7, (dtr in next 4 sc) worked off together into a Cluster, ** ch 13, remove hook, insert it back in 1st st of 13-ch, catch lp and pull thru, ch 1, (1 sc, 1 hdc, 8 dc, a 5-ch p, 8 dc, 1 hdc and 1 sc) in ring, * sl st in Cluster, ch 8, sl st in same sc on center, sl st in next 2 sc, ch 7, (dtr in next 4 sc) made into a Cluster, ch 13 and form a ring as before, ch 1, (1 sc, 1 hdc and 3 dc) in ring, sl st in 5th st up side of last ring, (5 dc, p, 8 dc, 1 hdc, 1 sc) in bal. of ring. Repeat from * around. Join 1st and last rings. Fasten off. **ROW 7**—Join to one p, (ch 23, sc in next p) 16 times. **ROW 8**—Sl st to 3d ch st, ch 5, dc in next 3d st, * ch 2, dc in next 3d st, ch 2, (dc, ch 5, dc) in next 3d (center) st, (ch 2, dc in next 3d st) 3 times, dc in 3d st of next lp, ch 2, dc in next 3d st. Repeat from * around. Sl st in 3d st of 1st 5-ch. **ROW 9**—Sl st to next 3d dc, 5 sc in next 5-ch, (ch 16, 5 sc in next point) 15 times, ch 16, sl st in 1st sc. **ROW 10**—Ch 6, (tr in next 4 sc) made into a Cluster, * ch 8, a 3-tr-Cluster in 8th st of next lp, ch 7, a 3-tr-Cluster in next st, ch 8, (tr in next 5 sc) made into a Cluster. Repeat from * around and join to 1st Cluster. **ROW 11**—(Ch 17, tr in 4th st of 7-ch lp between next 2 Clusters, ch 17, sc in next large Cluster) repeated around. **ROW 12**—Like Row 8 except 2 more sps on each side of points. Fasten off. **ROW 13**—5 sc in center sp of one point, (ch 26, 5 sc in next point) 15 times, ch 26, sl st in 1st sc. **ROW 14**—Ch 6, (tr in next 4 sc) made into a Cluster, * ch 12, a 3-tr-Cluster in 13th st of next lp, ch 7, a 3-tr-Cluster in next st, ch 12, (tr in next 5 sc) made into a Cluster. Repeat from * around. Join to 1st Cluster. **ROW 15**—Like Row 11 except with 20-chs. **ROW 16**—Like Row 8 except 3 more sps on each side of points. Fasten off. **ROW 17**—Like Row 13 but with 34-ch lps. **ROW 18**—Repeat Row 14 to *. ** Ch 16, a 3-tr-Cluster in 17th st of next lp, ch 7, a Cluster in next st, ch 16, (tr in next 5 sc) made into a Cluster. Repeat from ** around. Join to 1st Cluster. **ROW 19**—Like Row 11 but with 23-ch lps. **ROW 20**—Like Row 8 except 4 more sps on each side of points. **EDGE**—* (3 sc in next sp) 8 times, repeat Row 6 from ** to *. 3 sc in same sp, (3 sc in next sp) 7 times. Repeat from * around, join and fasten off. Stretch about 2" and pin right-side-down in a true circle. Steam and press dry thru a cloth.

Glory

**Materials Required: AMERICAN THREAD COMPANY
The Famous "PURITAN" MERCERIZED CROCHET
COTTON, Article 40**

1 ball White, Cream or Ecru or

**The Famous "PURITAN" STAR SPANGLED MER-
CERIZED CROCHET COTTON, Article 40**

3 balls Yellow Spangle or color of your choice
Steel crochet hook No. 7

Approximate size of doily: 14 inches in diameter.

Chain (ch) 6, join to form a ring, ch 3 and work 11 double crochet (d c) in ring, join in 3rd stitch (st) of ch.

2nd Round. Ch 3, d c in same space, 2 d c in each of the next 11 d c, join in 3rd st of ch.

3rd Round. Ch 7, skip 1 d c, d c in next d c, * ch 4, skip 1 d c, d c in next d c, repeat from * all around, ch 4, join in 3rd st of ch.

4th Round. Slip stitch (sl st) into loop, ch 3, 1 d c, ch 2, 2 d c in same space, * ch 2, 1 d c, ch 1, 1 d c in next loop, ch 2, 2 d c, ch 2, 2 d c (shell) in next loop, repeat from * all around ending with ch 2, 1 d c, ch 1, 1 d c in next loop, ch 2, join.

5th Round. Sl st to center of shell, ch 3, 1 d c, ch 2, 2 d c in same space, * ch 3, single crochet (s c) in next loop, ch 3, 1 d c, ch 1, 1 d c in next ch 1 space, ch 3, s c in next loop, ch 3, shell in next shell, repeat from * all around ending to correspond, ch 3, join.

6th Round. Sl st to center of shell, ch 3, 1 d c, ch 2, 2 d c in same space, * ch 5, skip 2 loops, 1 d c, ch 1, 1 d c in next ch 1 space, ch 5, skip 2 loops, shell in next shell, repeat from * all around ending to correspond, ch 5, join.

7th Round. Ch 3, * d c in next d c, 2 d c in center of

Continued on page 94

Lattice-edge Doily

Materials Required — AMERICAN THREAD COMPANY "STAR" MERCERIZED CROCHET COTTON,
Article 30, Size 50.

1—150 yd. Ball White.
Steel Crochet Hook No. 12 or 13.
Doily measures about 9½ inches.
Ch 8, join to form a ring, ch 4 and work 23 tr c into ring, join in 4th st of ch.
2nd Row. Ch 7, skip 2 tr c, s c in next tr c, repeat from * 6 times, ch 3, d c in same space with joining (this brings thread in position for next row).
3rd Row. * Ch 8, s c in next loop, repeat from * 6 times, ch 3, tr c in d c.
4th Row. * Ch 10, s c in next loop, repeat from * 6 times, ch 5, tr c in tr c.
5th Row. * Ch 8, s c in next loop, ch 8, s c in same loop, repeat from * 6 times, ch 8, s c in next loop, ch 4, tr c in tr c.
6th Row. * Ch 8, s c in next loop, repeat from * 14 times, ch 4, tr c in tr c.
7th Row. * Ch 9, s c in next loop, repeat from * 14 times, ch 5, tr c in tr c.
8th Row. * Ch 8, s c in next loop, ch 8, s c in same loop, repeat from * 14 times, ch 8, s c in next loop, ch 4, tr c in tr c.
9th Row. ** Ch 4, s c in next loop, ch 4, s c in next loop, * ch 15, s c in same loop, repeat from * 4 times, repeat from ** 15 times, join, break thread.

10th Row. Join thread in 1st 15 ch loop, * ch 7, s c in next loop, repeat from * 3 times, s c in next loop, then repeat from first * 14 times, * ch 7, s c in next loop, repeat from * twice, ch 3, tr c in next loop.
11th Row. ** S c in next loop, * ch 7, s c in next loop, repeat from * twice, repeat from ** 14 times, * ch 7, s c in next loop, repeat from *, ch 3, tr c in tr c.
12th Row. * Ch 7, s c in next loop, repeat from * 46 times, ch 3, tr c in tr c.
Next 2 Rows. Same as last row.
Next 2 Rows. Work in 8 ch loops ending each row with ch 4, tr c in tr c.
17th Row. Ch 3, 4 d c over loop, * 5 d c, ch 5, 5 d c over next loop, repeat from * all around ending row with 5 d c over 1st loop, ch 5, join in 3rd st of ch.
18th Row. Sl st to next 5 ch loop, ch 3, 2 d c in same loop, * ch 11, 3 d c in next 5 ch loop, repeat from * 46 times, ch 6, d tr c in 3rd st of ch, (d tr c: 3 times over needle).
19th Row. Ch 3, 2 d c over same loop, * ch 11, 3 d c in next loop, repeat from * 46 times, ch 6, d tr c in 3rd st of ch.
20th Row. Repeat last row but work 12 ch loops between groups of d c.
21st Row. Ch 3, 2 d c over same loop, * ch 11, sl st in 5th st from hook for picot, ch 6, sl st in 1st ch for picot, ch 5, sl st in 1st ch for picot, sl st in 1st picot, ch 6, 3 d c over next loop, repeat from * all around, working ch 6, 3 picot group, ch 6 to complete row, join, break thread.

Doily Drama

Materials Required — AMERICAN THREAD COMPANY "SILLATEEN" "SANSIL" or "STAR" PEARL COTTON Size 8, White or Colors.

3—60 Yard Balls or 124 Yards are required to make 1 doily.

Steel Crochet Hook Number 10.

Ch 10, join to form a ring, * ch 7, s c into ring, repeat from * 15 times (16 loops).

2nd Row. Sl st to center of loop, * ch 7, skip 1 loop, s c in next loop, repeat from * all around.

3rd Row. Sl st in center of loop, * ch 4, d c in 1st stitch of ch, ch 4, d c in 1st st of ch, s c in next loop repeat from * all around.

4th Row. Ch 7, d c in 4th st from hook, ch 4, d c in 1st st of ch, * sl st in top of next 2 petals, ch 4, d c in 1st st of ch, ch 4, d c in 1st st of ch, d c in s c of previous row, ch 4, d c in 1st st of ch, ch 4, d c in 1st st of ch, repeat from * all around, join in 3rd st of ch.

5th Row. Sl st to top of petal, * ch 4, d c in 1st st of ch, ch 4, d c in 1st st of ch, sl st in top of next 2 petals, repeat from * all around.

6th Row. Sl st to top of petal, ch 8, thread over needle, insert in top of next 2 petals, work off 2 loops, thread over needle, insert in same space and work off all loops 2 at a time, ch 3 and work 2 more 2 d c cluster sts in same space with ch 3 between, * ch 5, d c in top of next 2 petals, ch 5, 3—2 d c cluster sts with ch 3 between in top of next 2 petals, repeat from * all around, ch 5, join in 3rd st of ch 8.

7th Row. 5 s c in each loop.

8th Row. * Ch 5, skip 3 s c, s c in next s c, repeat from * all around (40 loops).

9th Row. Sl st to center of loop, * ch 5, s c in next loop, repeat from * all around.

Repeat 9th row 3 more times.

13th and 14th Rows. Same as previous row having 6 ch loops.

15th Row. 6 s c over each loop.

16th Row. Ch 3, d c in next s c, * ch 5, skip 4 s c, 1 d c in each of the next 2 s c, repeat from * all around, ch 5, join.

17th Row. Ch 3, d c in next d c, * ch 5, 1 d c in each of the next 2 d c, repeat from * all around, ch 5, join.

18th Row. Ch 3, d c in d c, * ch 3, s c over the 2 loops of previous rows, ch 3, 1 d c in each of the next 2 d c, repeat from * all around, ch 3, s c over the 2 loops of previous rows, ch 3, join.

19th Row. Ch 3, 1 d c between the 2 d c, 1 d c in next d c, * ch 3, skip 1 loop, 4 s c in next loop, 1 s c in d c, 4 s c in next loop, ch 3, 1 d c in next d c, 1 d c between the 2 d c, 1 d c in next d c, repeat from * all around, ch 3, skip 1 loop, 4 s c in next loop, 1 s c in d c, 4 s c in next loop, ch 3, join.

20th Row. Ch 3, * 2 d c in next d c, 1 d c in next d c, ch 3, skip 1 s c, 1 s c in each of the next 7 s c, ch 3, 1 d c in next d c, repeat from * all around.

21st Row. Ch 3, d c in next d c, * ch 2, 1 d c in each of the next 2 d c, 1 d c in next ch, ch 3, skip 1 s c, 1 s c in each of the next 5 s c, ch 3, skip 2 chs, 1 d c in next ch, 1 d c in each of the next 2 d c, repeat from * all

Continued on page 93

First Act

MATERIALS — Lily Skytone Mercerized Crochet Cotton:—1-ball in White or Ecru. Crochet hook size 10. Size—12".

Ch 9, sl st in 1st st. Ch 1, 16 sc in ring, sl st in 1st sc. (Ch 6, sc in next sc) 15 times, ch 3, dc in next sc. ROW 2—(Ch 6, sc in next lp) 15 times, ch 3, dc in dc at end of last row. Repeat Row 2 once. ROW 4—Ch 3, 2 dc in same lp, (ch 5, 3 dc in next lp) repeated around. End with ch 3, dc in top of 1st 3-ch. ROW 5—Turn, * ch 6, 4 tr in starting st of 6-ch, holding back the last lp of each tr on hook, thread over and pull thru all 5 lps on hook at once for a Cluster, ch 7, a 4-tr-Cluster in 6th ch st from hook, ch 1, sc in next 5-ch lp. Repeat from * around, ending with one Cluster, ch 1 and a 5-tr-Cluster made in st at base of 1st Cluster. ROW 6—Ch 1, turn, sc between last 2 Clusters, ch 12, sc between 2 Clusters of next lp, ** ch 5, turn, sk last 2 sts of 12-ch, dc in next st, * ch 2, dc in next 3d st. Ch 5, turn, sk last dc, dc in next dc, ch 2, dc in 3d st of next 5-ch, ** ch 6, sc between Clusters of next lp, ch 5, turn, sk last 2 sts of 6-ch, dc in next st. Repeat from * around. To complete row, sl st to 3d st of 1st lp, ch 2, turn, sk last 2 sts of last 6-ch, dc in next st, ch 2, dc in next 3d st, ch 5, turn, dc in next dc, ch 2, sl st in next 3d st of starting 12-ch lp. ROW 7—Sl st up to center st at top of next square, ch 3, 5 dc in same st, ch 3, turn, 2 dc in last dc, dc in each of next 4 dc, 3 dc in end st. Ch 3, turn, sk last 4 dc, tr in next dc, * (ch 3, tr) 3 times in same st, ch 3, sk 4 dc, sl st in end st. Ch 5, 6 dc in one lp of center st at top of next square, ch 3, turn, 2 dc in last dc, dc in next 4 dc, 2 dc in end dc, sl st in next 3d ch st. Ch 3, turn, sk sl st and last 3 dc, tr in next dc. Repeat from * around. Ch 2, sl st in corner of 1st triangle. ROW 8—* (3 sc in next 3-ch sp, 1 sc in tr) 4 times, 3 sc in next sp, 1 sc between triangles. Repeat from * around and join. ROW 9—Ch 20, sc in tip of next point and repeat from ** to ** in Row 6. * Ch 6, dtr down in sc between points, ch 5, turn, dc in 3d st of 6-ch, ch 2, dc in next 3d ch st, ch 5, turn, dc in next dc, ch 2, dc in 3d st of next 5-ch, ch 6, sc in tip of next point and make another square. Repeat from * around, joining final 6-ch to 8th st of 1st 20-ch, then complete row as in Row 6. ROW 10—Sl st to top corner of next square, * (ch 12, sc in 2 lps of 5th ch st from hook for a p) twice, ch 8, sc in top of next square. Repeat from * around. Cut 6" long, thread to a needle and fasten off on back. ROW 11—Sc in center of one lp, * (ch 7, p) 3 times, ch 3, sc in next lp. Repeat from * around and fasten off.

Stretch doily several inches and pin right-side-down in a true circle. Steam and press dry thru a cloth.

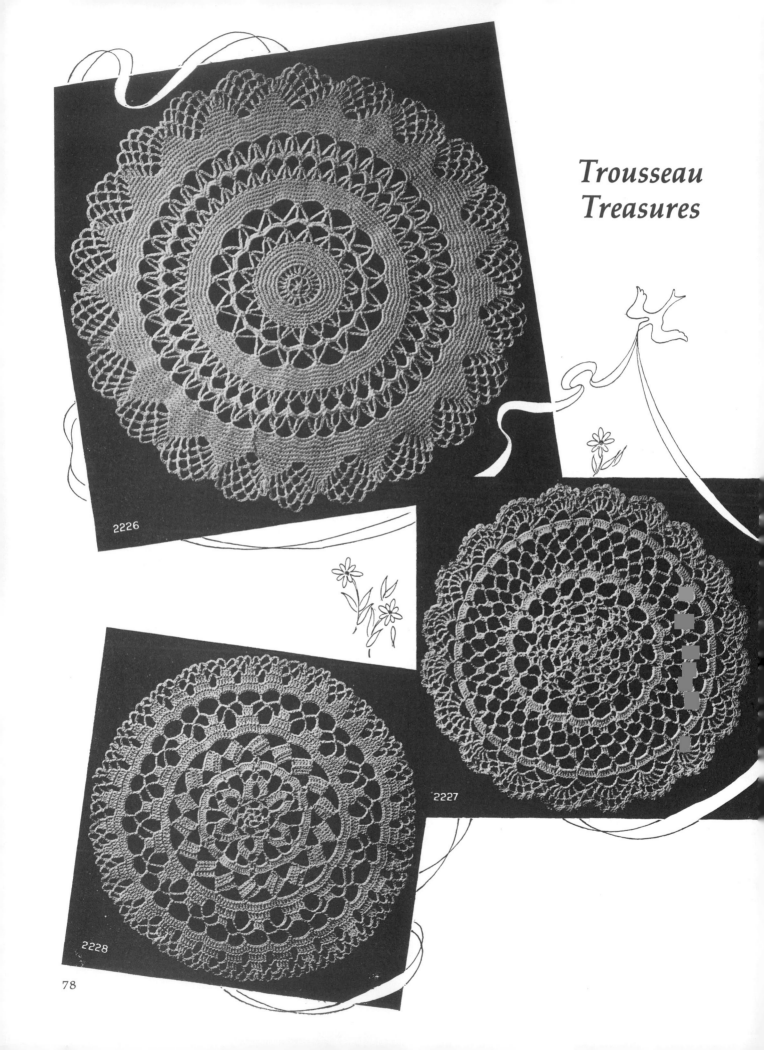

2226

2227

2228

DOILY No. 2226

Materials Required—AMERICAN THREAD COMPANY "PURITAN," "TROJAN," "DE LUXE" MERCERIZED CROCHET COTTON or "STAR" PEARL COTTON
Size 5

About 500 Yds. will make one Doily.
Steel Crochet Hook No. 9 or 10.
Doily measures about 13 inches.

Ch 6, d c in first st of ch, * ch 2, d c in same space, repeat from * 4 times, ch 2 and join in 4th st of ch 6.

2nd Row. 3 s c in each loop, join.

3rd Row. Ch 4, 1 d c in each s c with ch 1 between each d c (21 meshes).

4th Row. 2 s c in each space.

5th Row. Increase in every 3rd s c and work 1 row even.

7th Row. Increase in every 5th s c and work 2 rows even.

10th Row. Ch 4, skip 1 s c, tr c in next s c, ch 4, skip 1 s c, sl st in next s c, repeat from beginning all around ending row with tr c instead of ch.

11th Row. Ch 7, s c in next tr c, repeat from beginning all around.

12th Row. 9 s c over each loop.

13th Row. Ch 6, tr c in center of scallop, ch 6, sl st between scallops, repeat from beginning all around ending row with d tr c instead of ch.

14th Row. Ch 7, 3 s c over next tr c, repeat from beginning all around.

15th Row. 1 s c in each s c and 8 s c over each loop.

Next 5 Rows. 1 s c in each s c.

Repeat 10th and 11th rows.

Next Row. Work 7 s c over each loop, join, and repeat 13th row.

Next Row. Ch 6, s c in next tr c, repeat from beginning all around.

Next Row. 7 s c in each loop.

Next 5 Rows. 1 s c in each s c.

Next Row. 11 s c, * ch 7, skip 4 s c, 1 s c in each of the next 11 s c, repeat from * all around, ending last loop in 2nd s c of 1st group of s c. Work 8 more s c, ch 6, sl st into center of loop, ch 6, skip 1 s c, 1 s c in each of the next 9 s c, continue all around and work 4 more rows decreasing 1 s c each side of solid section and increasing 1 mesh each side of open section of scallop.

DOILY No. 2227

Materials Required—AMERICAN THREAD COMPANY "STAR" or "GEM" MERCERIZED CROCHET COTTON, Size 20 or 30

1—300 Yd. Ball White, Ecru, Cream or Colors.
Steel Crochet Hook No. 10 or 11.
Doily measures about 8 inches.

Ch 10, join to form a ring, ch 3, 19 d c in ring, join.

2nd Row. Ch 8, skip 1 d c, d c in next d c, * ch 4, skip 1 d c, d c in next d c, repeat from * all around, ch 4, join in 5th st of ch.

3rd Row. Ch 3, d c in same space, ch 3, 2 d c in same space, * ch 1, 2 d c in next d c, ch 3, 2 d c in same d c, repeat from * all around, ch 1, join.

4th Row. Sl st into center of shell, ch 3, d c in same space, ch 3, 2 d c in same space, * ch 3, 2 d c in next shell, 2 d c in same space, repeat from * all around, ch 3, join.

5th Row. Sl st into shell, ch 3, shell in shell, * ch 6, shell in next shell, repeat from * all around, ch 6, join.

6th Row. Sl st into shell, ch 6, d c in same space, * ch 3, d c in same space, repeat from *, ch 1, ** s c over 6 ch loop, ch 1, d c in next shell, * ch 3, d c in same shell, repeat from * twice, ch 1 and repeat from ** all around.

7th Row. 3 s c in each of the 3 ch loops, ch 8, 3 s c in each of the next 3 ch loops and continue all around.

8th Row. Sl st to center st of next group of s c, ch 3, d c in same space, * ch 7, 2 d c over next ch, ch 7, 2 d c in center s c of next group of s c, repeat from * all around.

9th Row. Ch 3 and work 9 d c over each loop.

10th Row. Ch 3, d c in same space, * ch 5, skip 3 d c, 1 d c in each of the next 3 d c, ch 5, 2 d c between groups of d c, repeat from * all around.

11th Row. Sl st to center of next ch, ch 10, d c in next ch, * ch 7, d c in next ch, repeat from * all around joining row in 3rd st of ch.

12th Row. Sl st to 3rd st of ch, ch 3, 2 d c over same ch, * ch 7, 2 d c over next ch, ch 7, 3 d c over next ch, repeat from * all around.

13th Row. Sl st to center of next ch, * ch 9, s c into next ch, repeat from * all around.

14th Row. Ch 3 and work 7 d c over each loop.

15th Row. Ch 9, s c between next 2 groups of d c, repeat all around.

16th Row. Sl st to 3rd st of loop, * 3 s c over loop, ch 2, and work 6 tr c with ch 2 between in next loop, ch 2, repeat from * all around.

17th Row. S c in center s c, ch 3 and d c in each tr c with ch 3 between, ch 3 and repeat from beginning all around.

18th Row. Sl st to 1st d c, * ch 4, d c in 4th st from hook, sl st in next d c, repeat from * all around.

CROCHETED DOILY No. 2228

Materials Required—AMERICAN THREAD COMPANY "SILLATEEN SANSIL"

2—60 Yd. Balls White or Colors.
Steel Crochet Hook No. 10 or 11.
Doily measures about 7 inches.

1st Row. Ch 6, join to form a ring, ch 5, d c into ring, * ch 3, d c in ring, repeat from * 3 times, ch 3, join to 3rd st of ch 5.

2nd Row. Slip st in loop, ch 3, d c in same place * ch 5, 2 d c in next loop, repeat from * 4 times, ch 5, join.

3rd Row. Slip st to center st of next loop, ch 14, sl st in same place, * ch 7, slip st in center st of next loop, ch 14, slip st in same place and repeat from * all around, ch 7, join.

4th Row. Slip st in 1st ch, ch 3, 1 d c in each of the next 6 chs, ch 5, 1 d c in each of the next 7 chs of same loop, sl st in center st of next loop and repeat all around (having 7 d c on each side of loop).

5th Row. Slip st to 4th d c, ch 8, * s c in loop, ch 5, s c in same loop, ch 6, skip 3 d c, 1 d c in next d c, ch 6, d c in center st of next group of d c, ch 6, repeat from * all around, join in 3rd st of ch.

Continued on page 81

Melody

**Materials Required — AMERICAN THREAD COM-
PANY "STAR" MERCERIZED CROCHET COTTON,
Article 20, Size 30.**

1—325 yd. Ball White or Ecru.
Steel Crochet Hook No. 12.
Doily measures about 13½ x 9½ inches.

Motif. Ch 6, join to form a ring, ch 5, d c in ring, * ch 2, d c in ring, repeat from * 5 times, ch 2, join in 3rd st of ch.

2nd Row. Sl st into mesh, ch 3, d c in same space, ch 3, cluster st in same space, (cluster st: thread over needle, insert in space and work off 2 loops, thread over needle, insert in same space and work off 2 loops, thread over and work off all loops at one time), ch 3, * 2 cluster sts with ch 3 between in next mesh, ch 3, repeat from * all around, join in top of 1st cluster st.

3rd Row. Sl st into loop, * ch 5, s c in next loop, repeat from * all around ending row with ch 2, d c in sl st (this brings thread in position for next row).

4th Row. * Ch 5, s c in next loop, repeat from * all around.

5th Row. Sl st into loop, ch 3, d c in same space, ch 4, sl st in 3rd st from hook for picot, ch 1, cluster st in same loop, * ch 4, s c in next loop, ch 3, sl st in top of s c just made for picot, ch 4, cluster st in next loop, ch 4, sl st in 3rd st from hook for picot, ch 1, cluster st in same loop, repeat from * all around ending row with ch 4, s c in next loop, picot, ch 4, join in 1st cluster st, break thread. Work a 2nd motif joining to 1st motif in last row as follows: sl st into loop, ch 3, d c in same space, ch 3, join to corresponding picot of 1st motif, ch 1, sl st in 2nd st of ch 3 to complete picot, ch 1, cluster st in same loop of 2nd motif, ch 4, s c in next loop, ch 2, join to next picot of 1st motif, ch 2, sl st in top of s c to complete picot, ch 4, cluster st in next loop, ch 3, join to next picot of 1st motif, ch 1, sl st in 2nd st of ch 3 to complete picot, ch 1, cluster st in same loop of 2nd motif and complete row same as 1st motif. Work a 3rd motif joining to 2nd motif in same manner leaving 2 scallops free at each side of 2nd motif, break thread. Attach thread in loop before center picot at end of work, * ch 7, s c in next loop, ch 7, skip the double cluster group, s c in next loop, repeat from * twice, ch 7, d c in next loop, tr c in joining of motifs, ch 5, tr c in same space, d c in next loop, * ch 7, s c in next loop, ch 7, skip the double cluster group, s c in next loop, repeat from * once, ch 7, d c in next loop, tr c in joining of motifs, ch 5, tr c in same space, d c in next loop, * ch 7, s c in next loop, ch 7, skip the double cluster group, s c in

Continued on next page

next loop, repeat from * 5 times, finish side to correspond.

2nd Row. Work 7 s c over each loop.

3rd Row. Ch 8, * d c in center of next scallop, ch 5, d c between scallops, ch 5, repeat from * 5 times. thread over needle twice, insert in center of next scallop and work off 2 loops, thread over needle twice, skip 3 s c, insert needle in next st and work off 2 loops twice, thread over and work off all loops at one time, ch 5, thread over needle twice, skip 6 s c, insert needle in next s c and work off 2 loops twice, thread over needle twice, skip 3 s c, insert needle in next s c and work off 2 loops twice, thread over and work off all loops at one time, * ch 5, d c between scallops, ch 5, d c in center of next scallop, repeat from * twice, ch 5, d c between scallops, ch 5, thread over needle twice, skip 3 s c, insert needle in next s c and work off 2 loops twice, thread over needle twice, skip 3 s c, insert needle in next s c and work off 2 loops twice, thread over and work off all loops at one time, ch 5, thread over needle twice, skip 6 s c, insert needle in next s c and work off 2 loops twice, thread over twice, skip 3 s c, insert needle in next s c and work off 2 loops twice, thread over and work off all loops at one time, ch 5, d c between scallops, ch 5, d c in center of next scallop, repeat from * all around working side same as opposite side.

4th Row. Work 5 s c in each loop.

5th Row. Sl st to center of scallop, ch 3, d c in same space, * ch 5, cluster st in center of next scallop, repeat from * all around, ch 5, join.

6th Row. Work 6 s c over each loop.

7th Row. Sl st to center of scallop, ch 3, 2 d c in same space, ch 5, s c in center of next scallop, * ch 5, 3 d c in center of next scallop, ch 5, s c in center of next scallop, repeat from * all around, ch 5, join.

8th Row. 1 s c in each of the 3 d c. * ch 9, 1 s c in each of the next 3 d c, repeat from * all around, * ch 9, join.

9th Row. Sl st to next s c, s c in same space. * ch 5, 3 d c in center st of next loop, ch 5, s c in center st of 3 s c group, repeat from * all around, join.

10th Row. Sl st to next d c and work same as 8th row but having 11 chs in each of the 8 loops around each end.

11th Row. Same as 9th row but having 6 ch loops before and after each 3 d c group.
Repeat the 10th and 11th rows.

14th Row. Ch 12, * s c in center st of 3 d c group, ch 8, tr c in next s c, ch 8, repeat from * all around, join in 4th st of ch.

15th Row. Work 9 s c over each of the next 8 loops, 7 s c over each of the next 15 loops, 9 s c over each of the next 19 loops, 7 s c over each of the next 15 loops, 9 s c over each of the next 11 loops.

16th Row. Sl st to center of scallop, * ch 9, s c in center of next scallop, repeat from * all around.

17th Row. Sl st to center of loop, ch 1, 3 s c in same space, ch 5, 2 cluster sts with ch 5 between in next loop, * ch 5, 3 s c in next loop, ch 5, 2 cluster sts with ch 5 between in next loop, repeat from * all around, ch 5, join.

18th Row. 1 s c in each of the next 3 s c, ch 5, skip 1 loop, 4 cluster sts with ch 2 between each cluster st in next loop, ch 5, repeat from beginning all around, join.

19th Row. Sl st to next s c, ch 1, s c in same space, ** ch 5, * 2 cluster sts with ch 2 between in next 2 ch loop, ch 2, repeat from *, 2 cluster sts with ch 2 between in next 2 ch loop, ch 5, s c in center st of 3 s c group, repeat from ** all around, join.

20th Row. Sl st between 1st 2 cluster sts, cluster st in same space, ** ch 5, sl st in 4th st from hook for picot, ch 1, cluster st in same space, * ch 6, sl st in 4th st from hook for picot, ch 2, skip 1 loop, cluster st in next loop, ch 5, sl st in 4th st from hook for picot, ch 1, cluster st in same space, repeat from *, ch 2, thread over needle, insert in next loop and work off 2 loops, thread over needle, insert in next loop and work off 2 loops, thread over and work off all loops at one time, ch 2, cluster st between next 2 cluster sts, repeat from ** all around, break thread.

Trousseau Treasures

Continued from page 79

6th Row. Slip st into loop, ch 3, 6 d c in same loop, * d c in 5 ch loop, ch 3, d c in same place, 7 d c in each of the next 3 loops, repeat from * all around, join and break thread.

7th Row. ** Ch 6, sl st in 3 ch loop, ch 3, turn, 6 d c on ch, ch 3, turn, 1 d c in each d c taking back loop of st only, * ch 6, sl st in between next two 7 d c groups, ch 3, turn, 6 d c on ch, ch 3, turn, 1 d c in each d c picking up back loop of st only and repeat from * then repeat from ** all around, join in 1st st of ch.

8th Row. Sl st to point, * ch 9, sl st in next point, repeat from * all around.

9th Row. Ch 3, 1 d c in each ch, d c in each point, repeat all around.

10th Row. Sl st to 2nd d c, ch 3, 1 d c in each of next 6 d c, * ch 9, skip 3 d c, 1 d c in each of the next 7 d c, repeat from * all around, there are 18—7 d c groups, ch 9, join.

11th Row. Sl st to 3rd d c, ch 3, d c in next d c, d c in same place, d c in next d c, * ch 6, s c in loop, ch 6, d c in 3rd d c, 2 d c in next d c, d c in next d c, repeat from * all around, ch 6, s c in loop, ch 6, join.

12th Row. Sl st to center of loop, ch 11, d c in next loop, * ch 8, d c in next loop, repeat from * all around, join in 3rd st of ch.

13th Row. Sl st to ch, ch 3, 1 d c in each ch, * skip the d c, 1 d c in each of the next 8 chs, repeat from * all around.

14th Row. Sl st to next d c, ch 3, 1 d c in each of the next 5 d c, * ch 5, skip 2 d c, 1 d c in each of the next 6 d c, repeat from * all around, join (there are 36 of 6 d c groups).

15th Row. Sl st to next d c, ch 3, 1 d c in each of the next 3 d c, * ch 5, s c in loop, ch 5, skip 1 d c, 1 d c in each of the next 4 d c, repeat from * all around, ch 5, s c in next loop, ch 5, join.

16th Row. Sl st to next d c, * ch 5, s c in next loop, ch 5, s c in next loop, ch 5, s c in center st of next d c group, repeat from * all around.

Rose Filet Centerpiece

MATERIALS REQUIRED:
DAISY Mercerized Crochet Cotton, Art. 65:—
2 skeins White size 30; or
DAISY Mercerized Crochet Cotton, Art. 97:—
3 balls White size 30; or
Lily MERCROCHET Cotton, Art. 161:—
3 balls White size 30; or
Lily SKY-TONE Mercerized Crochet Cotton, Art. 123:—
3 balls White.
Steel crochet hooks No. 13 with DAISY or MERCROCHET,
No. 10 with SKY-TONE.
SIZE:—With DAISY or MERCROCHET—17 to 19 inches;
with SKY-TONE—22 inches.
Starting at bottom of Chart, ch 44. ROW 1—Dc in 8th ch from hook (half-sp made), (ch 2, sk 2 ch, dc in next ch) 12 times (12 sps made), ch 2, tr in same place with last dc (half-sp added). ROW 2—Ch 22, turn, dc in 8th ch from hook, (ch 2, sk 2 ch, dc in next st) 5 times (1 half-sp and 5 sps added), ch 2, dc in next dc, (2 dc in next sp, dc in next dc) 12 times (12 blks made), ch 5, sk 2 ch, sl st in next ch, (ch 5, turn, dc in 3d st of previous ch-5) 5 times, ch 2, turn, tr in 3d st of last ch-5 (5 sps and 1 half-sp added).

Mark the right side of this row as right side of doily.
ROW 3—Ch 13, turn, dc in 8th ch from hook, (ch 2, sk 2 ch, dc in next st) twice (1 half-sp and 2 sps added), 1 sp, 7 blks, 10 sps

and 7 blks, ch 2, dc in 3d st of end ch-7, ch 5, dc in same st, ch 5, turn, dc in 3d st of previous ch-5, ch 2, turn, tr in 3d st of last ch-5 (2 sps and 1 half-sp added). ROW 4—Start and end as in last row. ROW 5—Add 1 half-sp and 2 sps, then make 1 sp, 4 blks, 13 sps, 1 blk, 1 sp, 1 blk, 12 sps, 4 blks, 1 sp and add 2 sps and 1 half-sp.

ROW 6—Ch 10, turn, dc in 8th ch from hook, ch 2, dc in next tr (1 half-sp and 1 sp added), make 1 sp, 4 blks, 11 sps, 3 blks, 1 sp, 4 blks, 1 sp, 2 blks, 12 sps and 4 blks. Ch 5, sl st in 3d st of end ch-7, ch 5, turn, dc in 3d st of previous ch-5, ch 2, turn, tr in 3d st of last ch-5 (1 sp and 1 half-sp added). ROWS 7, 8 and 9—Start and end each row as in Row 6. ROW 10—Ch 7, turn, dc in tr (1 half-sp added), 1 sp, 3 blks and follow Chart across, ending with 3 blks, 1 sp, ch 2, tr in same st with last dc (1 half-sp added). Follow Chart thru Row 19. ROW 20—Ch 5, turn, sk tr, dc in next dc (1 sp made), 2 blks and follow Chart across, ending with 1 sp even. Follow Chart thru Row 33. ROW 34—To make Lacet St Center, (ch 3, sk 2 dc, sc in next dc, ch 3, sk 2 dc, dc in next dc) 3 times (3 Lacet Sts made). Follow Chart across. ROW 35—Across Center, make 1 sp, ch 5, sk 5 dc, dc in next dc, (ch 5, dc in next dc) 3 times, ch 5, sk 5 dc, dc in next dc, 1 sp, 4 blks and follow Chart across. ROW 36—Across Center make 1 Lacet St, ch 3, sk 2 dc, sc in next dc, ch 3, dc in next dc, (ch 3, sc in next ch-5 sp, ch 3, dc in next dc) 5 times, ch 3, sc in next ch-5, ch 3, sk 2 dc, dc in next dc, make 1 more Lacet St, 3 blks and follow chart across. Follow Chart thru Row 60. ROW 61—Ch 4, turn, sk 1st dc, dc in next dc (half-sp decrease), follow Chart across, ending with 1 blk, 1 sp, tr in 3d st of end ch (half-sp decreased). Follow Chart thru Row 96. ROW 97 — Ch 1,

"ROSE FILET CENTERPIECE"

turn, sk tr, sl st across to 2d dc, ch 4, dc in next dc, 1 sp, 3 blks and follow Chart across. Follow Chart thru Row 108. In Rows 105 thru 108, ch 1, turn, sl st across to proper place to start each row.

EDGE—Ch 3 and work dc around doily, putting 2 dc in each ch-2 sp, 3 dc in each ch-4 sp and 1 dc in each st between sps. Join to top of ch-3. 2d rnd—Ch 1, (sc in 12 dc, ch 5, sl st in last sc for a p) repeated around, join and fasten off. Stretch and pin doily right-side-down in a true circle. Steam and press dry thru a cloth.

Cloverleaf

Doily measures 17 inches in diameter

J. & P. COATS BIG BALL BEST SIX CORD MERCERIZED CROCHET, Art. A.104, Size 30: 2 balls of White, or

CLARK'S BIG BALL MERCERIZED CROCHET, Art. B.34, Size 30: 2 balls of White.

Milwards Steel Crochet Hook No. 10.

Starting at Center, ch 4. **1st rnd:** 3 dc in 4th ch from hook, ch 3, sc in same ch, (ch 3, 3 dc in same ch, ch 3, sc in same ch) 3 times (4 petals). **2nd rnd:** Sl st to center dc of first petal, ch 14, * dc in center dc of next petal, ch 11. Repeat from * around. Join to 3rd ch of ch-14. **3rd rnd:** Ch 5, dc in same place as sl st, * (ch 2, skip 1 ch, dc in next ch) 5 times; ch 2, in next dc make dc, ch 2 and dc. Repeat from * around, ending with ch 2, sl st in 3rd ch of ch-5 (28 sps). **4th rnd:** Ch 18, * skip 1 dc, d tr in next dc, ch 13. Repeat from * around. Join to 5th ch of ch-18. **5th rnd:** Sc in same place as sl st, * ch 7, sc in center ch of next loop, ch 7, sc in next d tr. Repeat from * around. Join to first sc. **6th rnd:** Sc in same place as sl st, * ch 7, sc in next sc. Repeat from * around. Join and break off. **7th rnd:** Attach thread to sc at any point, sc in same place, * ch 9, sc in next sc of next point. Repeat from * around. Join to first sc. **8th rnd:** Ch 5, * in next sp make (dc, ch 2) 4 times; dc in next sc, ch 2. Repeat from * around. Join to 3rd ch of ch-5 (70 sps). Now work flowers in strips as follows:

FIRST STRIP . . . Ch 4, 2 dc in 4th ch from hook making last 2 loops of last dc loose (this is center of flowers), ch 1, sc in top of last dc made, ch 3, in same place make 3 dc, ch 3, sc, ch 3 and 2 dc; ch 5, 2 tr in 5th ch from hook, making last 2 loops of last tr loose for center, ch 1, sc in top of last tr made, ch 4, in same place make 3 tr, ch 4, sc, ch 4 and 2 tr; ch 6, 2 d tr in 6th ch from hook, making last 2 loops of last d tr loose for center, ch 1, sc in top of last d tr made, (ch 5, in same place make 3 d tr, ch 5 and sc) 3 times; ch 5, d tr in same place, sl st at base of first ch-6 made (Large Flower completed); ch 4, tr in same place as last sl st, in center of next flower make sc, ch 4, 3 tr, ch 4, sc, ch 4 and tr; sl st at base of first ch-5 (Middle Flower completed); ch 3, dc in same place as sl st, in center of next flower make sc, ch 3, 3 dc, ch 3, sc, ch 3 and dc; sl st in same place as first sl st (Small Flower completed).

SECOND STRIP . . . (Sl st in next 2 ch and next dc of 8th rnd) 3 times; ch 4, dc in 4th ch from hook, ch 1, sc in top of last dc made, ch 3, 2 dc in same place, sl st in center dc of corresponding petal on Small Flower of First Strip, in same place on Second Strip make dc, ch 3, sc, ch 3 and 2 dc; ch 5, 2 tr in 5th ch from hook, in top of last tr make sc, ch 4, 2 tr, sl st in center tr of corresponding petal on Middle Flower of First Strip; in same place on Second Strip make tr, ch 4, sc, ch 4 and 2 tr; ch 6, 2 d tr in 6th ch from hook, in top of last d tr make sc, ch 5 and 2 d tr; sl st in center d tr of corresponding petal on Large Flower of First Strip, in same place on Second Strip make d tr, ch 5 and sc. Complete Large Flower, then complete other half of Strip as before, ending with sl st in same dc on center.

THIRD STRIP . . . (Sl st in next 2 ch and next dc of 8th rnd) twice; work as for Second Strip.

Then repeat Second and Third Strips alternately, joining Last Strip to First Strip. Sl st across to end of 8th rnd. Join and break off (28 strips).

Now work in rnds as follows: **1st rnd:** Attach thread to center d tr of any free petal, sc in same place, * ch 15, sc in center d tr of next free petal. Repeat from * around. Join. **2nd rnd:** Ch 3, dc in each ch and in each sc around. Join. **3rd rnd:** Ch 5, d tr in same place as sl st, * ch 23, skip 15 dc, holding back on hook the last loop of each d tr, make 2 d tr in next dc, thread over and draw through all loops on hook (cluster made). Repeat from * around. Join. **4th rnd:** Sc in same place as sl st, * ch 11, sc in center ch of ch-23, ch 11, sc in next cluster. Repeat from * around. Join. **5th rnd:** Sc in same place as sl st, * ch 11, sc in next sc. Repeat from * around. Join. **6th rnd:** Sl st in each ch and in next sc, sc in same place as last sl st, * ch 20, sc in sc of next point. Repeat from * around. Join. **7th rnd:** Ch 3, dc in each ch and in each sc around. Join. **8th rnd:** Ch 5, 6 d tr in same place as sl st, * ch 6, skip 5 dc, sc in next dc, (ch 11, skip 5 dc, sc in next dc) 5 times; ch 6, skip 5 dc, 7 d tr in next dc. Repeat from * around. Join.

9th rnd: Ch 5, d tr in next 2 d tr, * ch 3, tr in next d tr, ch 3, d tr in next 3 d tr, ch 6, sc in next ch-11 loop, (ch 11, sc in next loop) 4 times; ch 6, d tr in next 3 d tr. Repeat from * around. Join. **10th rnd:** Ch 5, d tr in next 2 d tr, * (ch 3, tr in next sp) twice; ch 3, d tr in next 3 d tr, ch 6, sc in next ch-11 loop, (ch 11, sc in next loop) 3 times; ch 6, d tr in next 3 d tr. Repeat from * around. Join. **11th rnd:** Ch 5, d tr in next 2 d tr, * (ch 4, tr in next sp) 3 times; ch 4, d tr in next 3 d tr, ch 6, sc in next ch-11 loop, (ch 11, sc in next loop) twice; ch 6, d tr in next 3 d tr. Repeat from * around. Join. **12th rnd:** Ch 5, d tr in next 2 d tr, * (ch 5, tr in next sp) 4 times; ch 5, d tr in next 3 d tr, ch 6, sc in next ch-11 loop, ch 11, sc in next loop, ch 6, d tr in next 3 d tr. Repeat from * around. Join. **13th rnd:** Ch 5, d tr in next 2 d tr, * (ch 6, tr in next sp) 5 times; ch 6, d tr in next 3 d tr, ch 6, sc in next ch-11 loop, ch 6, d tr in next 3 d tr. Repeat from * around. Join. **14th rnd:** Ch 7, holding back on hook the last loop of each long tr make a long tr (thread over 6 times) in next 2 d tr, thread over and draw through all loops on hook (cluster made); * (ch 8, tr in next sp) 6 times; ch 8, (make a long-tr cluster over next 3 d tr) twice. Repeat from * around. Join to tip of first cluster. **15th rnd:** Sl st to center of next loop, ch 12, * tr in next sp, ch 8. Repeat from * around. Join to 4th ch of ch-12 (98 sps). **16th rnd:** Ch 3, * 7 dc in next sp, dc in next tr. Repeat from * around. Join. **17th rnd:** Ch 5, d tr in same place as sl st, * ch 21, skip 13 dc, make a 2-d tr cluster in next dc. Repeat from * around. Join (58 sps). **18th rnd:** Sc in same place as sl st, * ch 11, sc in center of ch-21, ch 11, sc in tip

of next cluster. Repeat from * around. Join. **19th rnd**: Sc in same place as sl st, * ch 11, sc in next sc. Repeat from * around. Join. **20th rnd**: Sl st in each ch and in next sc, sc in same place as last sl st, * ch 15, sc in sc of next point. Repeat from * around. Join. **21st rnd**: Ch 4, * 17 tr in next loop, tr in next sc. Repeat from * around. Join and break off. Starch lightly and press.

Love at First Sight

MATERIALS:

J. & P. COATS or CLARK'S O.N.T.
BEST SIX CORD MERCERIZED CRO-
CHET, size 30:

SMALL BALL:
J. & P. COATS —2 balls of White,
Ecru or any color,
OR
CLARK'S O.N.T.—3 balls of White,
Ecru or any color.

BIG BALL:
J. & P. COATS —1 ball of White or
Ecru.

Steel Crochet Hook No. 10.

Doily measures 9½ x 15½ inches.

GAUGE: 5 sps make 1 inch; 5 rows
make 1 inch.

Starting at bottom of chart, ch 18.
1st row: Dc in 4th ch from hook, dc
in 14 ch (5 bls). Ch 5, turn. **2nd row:**
Dc in 4th ch from hook, dc in next ch
(1 bl increased), dc in 4 dc (bl over
bl), ch 2, skip 2 dc, dc in next dc (sp
over bl made), dc in 3 dc, ch 2, skip
2 dc, dc in next 3 dc, then make a
foundation dc as follows: Thread over,
insert hook in top st of turning ch and
draw loop through; thread over and
draw through 1 loop—*1 ch st made,
to be used as a foundation st for next
dc*—complete dc in usual manner. Make
2 more foundation dc and 1 dc in usual
way (1 bl increased). Ch 20, turn. **3rd
row:** Dc in 4th ch from hook, dc in
16 ch, (1 bl, 1 sp) 3 times; dc in
2 dc, foundation dc in top of turning
ch, 17 more foundation dc and 1 dc
in usual way. Ch 11, turn. **4th row:**
Dc in 4th ch from hook, dc in 7 ch,
6 sps, 2 bls, 1 sp, 1 bl, 1 sp, 2 bls,
5 sps, ch 2, foundation dc in top st of
turning ch, 8 more foundation dc and
1 dc in usual way. Ch 5, turn.

5th and 6th rows: Follow chart.
Ch 23, turn. **7th row:** Dc in 4th ch
from hook, dc in 19 ch, 1 bl, 11 sps,
1 bl, ch 5, skip 1 bl and 1 sp, dc in
next dc (bar), 1 sp, 1 bl, 11 sps, 2 dc,
foundation dc in top st of turning ch,
20 more foundation dc and 1 dc in
usual way. Ch 8, turn. **8th row:** 2 bls,
(1 sp, 1 bl) 4 times; 9 sps, 2 bls, 1 sp,
ch 5, dc in center ch of bar below, ch 5,
skip 3 dc, dc in next dc (2 bars),
2 bls, 9 sps, (1 bl, 1 sp) 4 times; inc
2 bls. Ch 8, turn. Starting with 9th
row, follow chart until the 26th row is
completed. Do not ch to turn at end of
26th row. **27th row:** Sl st in next 3 dc,
ch 3, and follow chart to within last bl
(1 bl decreased at both ends). Now
follow chart to top to complete doily.
Fasten off.
Starch lightly and press.

There are 10 spaces
between heavy lines

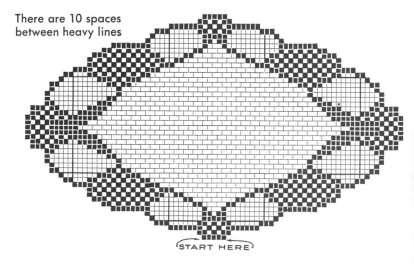

(START HERE)

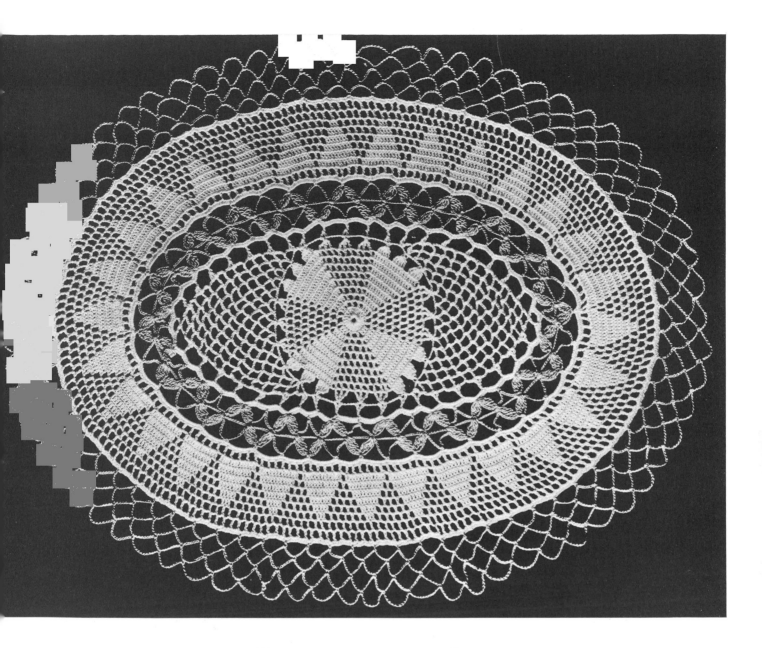

Pretty as a Peach

Materials: Clark's O.N.T. or J. & P. Coats Mercerized Crochet, Size 30, 1 ball each of White and 88 Peach. Milward's steel crochet hook No. 9.

With White, ch 8, join with sl st to form ring. **1st rnd:** Ch 4, 23 tr in ring. Join with sl st to 4th st of ch-4. **2nd rnd:** Ch 3, d c in each of next 2 sts, * ch 2, d c in next st, ch 2, skip 1 st, d c in next, ch 2, d c in each of next 3 sts. Repeat from * around, ending with ch 2, sl st to 3rd st of ch-3. **3rd rnd:** Ch 3, d c in top of ch-3 of previous rnd, * d c in each d c, 1 d c under ch-2, ch 2, d c in same place as last d c, ** ch 2, d c under next group of ch-2, repeat from ** into each sp of previous rnd, 1 d c in same place as last d c, repeat from * around, ending with ch 2, sl st to top of ch-3 at beginning of rnd. This makes 2 more d c in each group and 1 more sp.

4th to 9th rnds incl: Same as 3rd rnd. The 9th rnd will have 17 d c and 10 sps in each section. **10th rnd:** Ch 5, make one 4-tr cluster working over next 4 d c. * Ch 7, skip 1 d c, 5-tr cluster working over next 5 d c *. Repeat from * to * once. ** Ch 7, 3-tr cluster over next 3 d c **. Repeat from ** to ** twice. Repeat from * to * 3 times across solid portions and ** to ** 3 times across sps. End rnd with ch 7, sl st in 1st cluster.

11th rnd: Sl st to center of 1st ch-7, ch 8, 1 s c in next cluster, * ch 8, s c under ch-7, ch 8, s c in next cluster. Repeat from * until there are 14 loops, then turn, and work over these loops only. **Next row:** Sl st to center of 1st loop, * ch 8, s c under next loop, repeat from * across. (This makes 1 less loop

Continued on page 88

Sunburst

MATERIALS:

J. & P. Coats Best Six Cord Mercerized Crochet, Art. A.104, Size 30: 2 balls of White . . . Milwards Steel Crochet Hook No. 10.

See Thread Selection Chart—Page 2

Centerpiece measures 20 inches in diameter.

Starting at center, ch 6. Join with sl st to form ring. **1st rnd:** Ch 3, 11 dc in ring. Join with sl st to top of ch-3. **2nd rnd:** Ch 3, dc in same place as sl st, 2 dc in each dc around. Join. **3rd rnd:** Ch 3, * 2 dc in next dc (1 dc increased), dc in next dc. Repeat from * around. Join. **4th rnd:** Ch 3, * 2 dc in next dc, dc in next 2 dc. Repeat from * around. Join. **5th rnd:** Ch 3, dc in each dc around, increasing 12 dc evenly around and keeping increases over previous increases. Join. **6th to 12th rnds incl:** Ch 3, work as for 5th rnd, having 1 more dc on each rnd between increases and keeping increases in line (counting the ch 3 as 1 dc—there are 144 sts on 12th rnd, 10 dc between increases). **13th rnd:** Ch 3, dc in next 11 dc, * ch 1, dc in next 12 dc. Repeat from * around, ending with ch 1. Join. **14th rnd:** Sl st in next dc, ch 3, dc in next 10 dc, * ch 1, dc in ch-1 sp, ch 1, skip next dc, dc in next 11 dc. Repeat from * around. Join. **15th rnd:** Sl st in next dc, ch 3, * dc in each dc of this section to next ch-1 sp, (ch 1, dc in next sp) twice; ch 1, skip first dc of next dc section. Repeat from * around. Join. **16th to 24th rnds incl:** Work as for 15th rnd, having 1 sp more between dc-groups and 1 dc less on each dc section (1 dc left on each section on 24th rnd). **25th and 26th rnds:** Sl st in next sp, ch 5, * tr in next sp, ch 1. Repeat from * around. Join with sl st to 4th ch of ch-5. **27th rnd:** Sl st in next ch, ch 3, dc in same place as sl st, * 3 dc in next sp, 2 dc in next sp. Repeat from * around. Join. **28th rnd:** Ch 7, * skip next 3 dc, dc in next dc, ch 4. Repeat from * around. Join to 4th ch of ch-7. **29th, 30th and 31st rnds:** Sl st to center of sp, ch 7, * dc in next sp, ch 4. Repeat from * around. Join to 4th ch of ch-7. **32nd rnd:** Sl st in next sp, ch 3, 4 dc in same sp, 5 dc in each sp around. Join. **33rd rnd:** Sc in same place as sl st, * ch 5, skip 3 dc, sc in next dc. Repeat from * around. Join. **34th and 35th rnds:** Sl st to center of next loop, * ch 5, sc in next loop. Repeat from * around. Join. **36th, 37th and 38th rnds:** Work as for 34th rnd, making ch-6 loops instead of ch-5. Join (112 loops on 38th rnd). **39th rnd:** Sl st in next loop, ch 6, 7 d tr in same loop, * ch 7, skip next loop, 8 d tr in next loop. Repeat from * around. Join to top of ch-6. **40th rnd:** Sl st in next d tr, ch 6, * d tr in each d tr on this section, ch 7, skip first d tr of next section. Repeat from * around. **41st to 46th rnds incl:** Repeat 40th rnd, having 1 more ch on each rnd between d tr sections. Join (13 ch on 46th rnd). At end of 46th rnd, join and break off.

Starch lightly and press.

Pretty as a Peach
Continued from page 87

than last row.) Repeat this row until 1 loop remains. Fasten off. Attach thread to center of ch-7 between 1st 2 clusters of 5-tr on other side of circle, work to correspond from 11th rnd on. Do not fasten off after last loop is made. **12th rnd:** Sl st to center of last loop. Ch 11, * begin a tr tr over end of next row, draw through 2 loops, then thread over hook, insert hook under next loop and draw through. Then work off loops 2 at a time until all loops are off hook. Ch 7, repeat from *. At the sides, work the **tr tr** sts, drawing through sps at each side of the clusters in the 10th rnd. Continue to the single loop at other end of oval. After ch 7, make tr in center of this single loop, ch 5, 1 tr in same place as last st, then ch 7, and continue around, ending with 1 tr in center loop, ch 5, sl st to 4th st of ch at beginning of rnd. **13th rnd:** Ch 2, under each ch-7 loop work 9 s c. At end of rnd, sl st to 1st st and fasten off. **14th rnd:** Attach Peach to 5th s c of a 9-s c group. * Ch 7, 3-tr tr cluster in 5th s c of next s c-group, ch 7, 1 s c in same st, ch 7, another 3-tr tr cluster in same place, ch 7, 1 s c in 5th s c of next group. Repeat from * around.

15th rnd: Sl st to top of 1st cluster, * ch 8, 1 s c in next cluster, repeat from * around. Sl st to 1st ch at beginning of round.

16th rnd: * Ch 14, skip ch 8, 1 s c in next s c, ch 7, 3 tr tr cluster in same s c, skip ch 8, 3 tr tr-cluster in next s c, ch 7, s c in same s c, repeat from * around. Fasten off. **17th rnd:** Attach White to top of 2 clusters, * ch 9, 1 s c under ch-14 loop, ch 9, 1 s c between 2 clusters, repeat from * around. Sl st to 1st st. **18th rnd:** Ch 2, 12 s c under each ch-9 loop. **19th rnd:** Ch 5, 1 d c in 3rd s c, * ch 2, skip 2 sts, d c in next, repeat from * around, ending with ch 2, sl st to 3rd st of ch-5 (170 sps).

20th rnd: Ch 3, * 2 d c in next sp, 1 d c in d c, repeat from * 3 times (4 bls). Ch 2, 1 d c in next d c (1 sp), repeat from * around, ending with ch 2, sl st in 3rd st of ch-3. **21st rnd:** Sl st into 1st d c. Ch 3, d c in each of next 10 d c, * ch 2, d c in sp, ch 2, skip 1st d c, d c in each of next 11 d c, repeat from * around, ending with ch 2, sl st to 3rd st of ch-3. **22nd to 26th rnds incl:** Same as 21st, but make 2 less d c in each group and 1 more sp each rnd. The 26th rnd will have 1 d c at top of triangle of d c.

27th rnd: Rnd of sps. **28th rnd:** Ch 2, 3 s c in each sp, ending with sl st to ch-2. Fasten off. **29th rnd:** Attach Peach to 2nd s c of 1st 3-s c group. * Ch 12, skip 2 groups of 3 s c, s c in 2nd st of next group, repeat from * around. **30th and 31st rnds:** Sl st to top of 1st ch-12 loop, * ch 12, s c under next loop, repeat from * around. Fasten off.

Sunburst

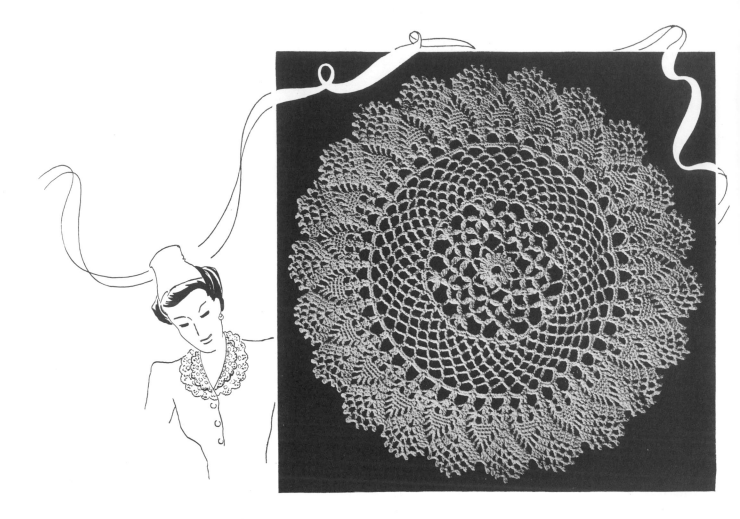

Frost Fair

**Materials Required—AMERICAN THREAD COMPANY
"SILLATEEN SANSIL" or "STAR" PEARL COTTON
Size 8, White or Colors**

3—60 Yd. Balls or 124 yards are required to make 1 Doily.
Steel Crochet Hook No. 10.
Doily measures about 9 inches.

Ch 10, join to form a ring, * ch 7, s c into ring, repeat
from * 15 times (16 loops).

2nd Row. Sl st to center of loop, * ch 7, skip 1 loop, s c
in next loop, repeat from * all around.

3rd Row. Sl st in center of loop, * ch 4, d c in 1st stitch
of ch, ch 4, d c in 1st st of ch, s c in next loop, repeat
from * all around.

4th Row. Ch 7, d c in 4th st from hook, ch 4, d c in 1st st
of ch, * sl st in top of next 2 petals, ch 4, d c in 1st st of
ch, ch 4, d c in 1st st of ch, d c in s c of previous row, ch
4, d c in 1st st of ch, ch 4, d c in 1st st of ch, repeat from *
all around, join in 3rd st of ch.

5th Row. Sl st to top of petal, * ch 4, d c in 1st st of ch,
ch 4, d c in 1st st of ch, sl st in top of next 2 petals,
repeat from * all around.

6th Row. Sl st to top of petal, ch 8, thread over needle,
insert in top of next 2 petals, work off 2 loops, thread
over needle, insert in same space and work off all loops
2 at a time, ch 3 and work 2 more 2 d c cluster sts in same

space with ch 3 between, * ch 5, d c in top of next 2
petals, ch 5, 3—2 d c cluster sts with ch 3 between in top
of next 2 petals, repeat from * all around, ch 5, join in
3rd st of ch 8.

7th Row. 5 s c in each loop.

8th Row. * Ch 5, skip 3 s c, s c in next s c, repeat from *
all around (40 loops).

9th Row. Sl st to center of loop, * ch 5, s c in next loop,
repeat from * all around. Repeat 9th row 3 more times.

13th and 14th Rows. Same as previous row having 6 ch
loops.

15th Row. 6 s c over each loop.

16th Row. Ch 3, d c in next s c, * ch 5, skip 4 s c, 1 d c
in each of the next 2 s c, repeat from * all around, ch 5,
join.

17th Row. Ch 3, d c in next d c, * ch 5, 1 d c in each of
the next 2 d c, repeat from * all around, ch 5, join.

18th Row. Ch 3, d c in d c, * ch 3, s c over the 2 loops of
previous rows, ch 3, 1 d c in each of the next 2 d c, repeat
from * all around, ch 3, s c over the 2 loops of previous
rows, ch 3, join.

19th Row. Ch 3, 1 d c between the 2 d c, 1 d c in next
d c, * ch 3, skip 1 loop, 4 s c in next loop, 1 s c in d c,
4 s c in next loop, ch 3, 1 d c in next d c, 1 d c between

Continued on page 93

Monticello

MATERIALS: For best results use—

CLARK'S O.N.T. OR J. & P. COATS

BEST SIX CORD MERCERIZED CROCHET, Size 30:

SMALL BALL:

CLARK'S O.N.T.—*2 balls of White or Ecru, or 3 balls*
OR *of any color.*

J. & P. COATS—*2 balls of White, Ecru, or any color.*

BIG BALL:

CLARK'S O.N.T.—*1 ball of White or Ecru.*
OR

J. & P. COATS—*1 ball of White, Ecru or any color.*

MILWARD'S *steel crochet hook No. 9.*

Completed large doily measures about 14½ inches in diameter; small doilies measure about 11½ inches in diameter.

LARGE DOILY... Ch 7, join with sl st. **1st rnd:** 14 s c in ring. Join. **2nd rnd:** Ch 6 (to count as tr and ch-2), * tr in next s c, ch 2. Repeat from * around; join to 4th st of ch-6 (14 sps). **3rd rnd:** S c in ch-2 sp, * ch 4, s c in next sp. Repeat from * around, ending with ch 2, d c in 1st s c made. **4th rnd:** * Ch 5, s c in next loop. Repeat from * around, ending with ch 2, d c in d c at base of 1st ch-5. **5th rnd:** Ch 12 (to count as tr and ch-8), * tr in next loop, ch 8. Repeat from * around, ending with ch 5, d c in 4th st of ch-12.

6th rnd: S c in loop (under bar of d c), * ch 5, s c in next loop, ch 4, s c in same loop. Repeat from * around, ending with ch 5, s c in last loop, ch 2, d c in 1st s c. **7th rnd:** * Ch 6, s c in next loop. Repeat from * around, ending with ch 3, d c at base of 1st ch-6. **8th rnd:** Ch 10 (to count as tr and ch-6), * tr in next loop, ch 6. Repeat from * around, ending with ch 3, d c in 4th st of ch-10. *Hereafter it is wise to mark beginning of rnds with a colored thread.* **9th rnd:** S c in loop (under d c), * ch 7, s c in next loop, ch 3, 3 tr in same loop, holding back the last loop of each tr on hook; thread over and draw through all loops on hook; ch 1 tightly (cluster). Ch 3, s c in next loop. Repeat from * around, ending with 3-tr cluster, tr in 1st s c. **10th rnd:** S c in top of tr just made, ch 3, 3-tr cluster under last tr made, * ch 4, s c in next loop, ch 8, s c in tip of next cluster of previous rnd, ch 3, 3-tr cluster under ch-3 following cluster. Repeat from * around, ending with ch 4, tr in s c at base of 1st ch-3. **11th rnd:** S c in top of last tr made, * ch 9, s c in tip of next cluster, ch 4, a 3-d tr cluster under next ch-4 (work as for previous clusters, making d tr instead of tr). Ch 4, s c in ch-8 loop. Repeat from * around, ending with 3-d tr cluster under ch-4, tr in 1st s c. **12th rnd:** S c in top of last tr made, ch 4, 3-d tr cluster in sp under tr; * ch 5, s c in next loop, ch 10, s c in tip of next cluster, ch 4, 3-d tr cluster under

Continued on page 93

Star of Them All

MATERIALS—DAISY Mercerized Crochet Cotton, size 30:—3-balls White, Cream or Ecru. Crochet hook size 12.

SMALL DOILY—(14″)—Ch 8, sl st in 1st st. Ch 4, dc in ring, (ch 1, dc in ring) 10 times, ch 1, sl st in 3d st of 1st 4-ch. **ROW 2**—Ch 3, turn, 1 dc in same st with sl st, (ch 3, a 2-dc-Cluster in next dc) 11 times, ch 3, sl st in 1st dc. **ROW 3**—Ch 3, turn, 1 dc in same st with sl st, (ch 5, a 2-dc-Cluster in next Cluster) 11 times, ch 5, sl st in 1st dc. Repeat Row 3 thru Row 6, with ch lps 2 sts longer in each row. Make Row 7 with 14-ch lps, then 6 rows with lps 2 sts longer in each row (26-ch lps in Row 13). **ROW 14**—Ch 5, turn, a 2-dc-Cluster in same st. * Ch 5, a 2-dc-Cluster in 5th st from hook, ch 6, a Cluster in 5th st from hook (a double-Cluster lp). A 3-dc-Cluster in same st with 1st Cluster, ch 22, a 3-dc-Cluster in next Cluster. Repeat from * around and join to 1st Cluster. **ROW 15**—Ch 5, turn, a 2-dc-Cluster in same st, * ch 18, a 3-dc-Cluster in next Cluster, ch 5, a 2-dc-Cluster in 5th ch st from hook, a 3-dc-Cluster in 1-ch between next 2 Clusters, make a double-Cluster lp, then a 3-dc-Cluster in same 1-ch, ch 5, a 2-dc-Cluster in 5th ch st from hook, a 3-dc-Cluster in end Cluster. Repeat from * around and join to 1st Cluster. **ROW 16**—Ch 5, turn, a 2-dc-Cluster in same st, * (ch 5, a 2-dc-Cluster in 5th ch st from hook, a 3-dc-Cluster between next 2 Clusters) repeated to tip of point, make a double-Cluster lp, then a 3-dc-Cluster in same center st, (ch 5, a 2-dc-Cluster in 5th ch st from hook, a 3-dc-Cluster between next 2 Clusters) repeated to end Cluster. ** Ch 14, a 3-dc-Cluster in next Cluster. Repeat from * around and join. **ROW 17**—Ch 5, turn, a 2-dc-Cluster in same st, (ch 10, a 3-dc-Cluster in next Cluster. Repeat Row 6 from * to **) repeated around and join. **ROW 18**—Repeat Row 16 with 5-ch lps. **ROW 19**—Repeat Row 17 without any ch-lps between points. Fasten off.

LACY POINTS—Turn and join between 1st 2 Clusters up left side of one point, ch 6, tr across between 1st 2 Clus-

ters on next point, ch 6, tr between next 2 Clusters. Ch 10, turn, sk last tr, tr in next tr, tr between next 2 Clusters on point, ch 5, dtr between next 2 Clusters. Ch 8, turn, a 3-dtr-Cluster in 5th st of center 10-ch, ch 8, a 3-dtr-Cluster in next st. Ch 8, tr in next tr, dtr between next 2 Clusters on point, ch 5, dtr between next 2 Clusters. Ch 8, turn, a Cluster in 3d st of 8-ch between center Clusters, (ch 8, a Cluster in next st) 3 times, ch 8, tr in next tr, dtr between next 2 Clusters on point, ch 5, dtr between next 2 Clusters. Ch 8, turn, a Cluster in 4th st of 8-ch between next 2 Clusters, ch 8, a Cluster in 3d st of next lp, (ch 8, a Cluster in next st) 3 times, ch 8, a Cluster in 5th st of next lp, ch 8, tr in next tr, dtr between next 2 Clusters on point. * Fasten off. Repeat between all points. Turn and join to tip of one point, ** ch 9, dtr in next tr, (ch 9, a Cluster in 4th st between next 2 Clusters) twice, ch 9, a Cluster in 3d st of next lp, (ch 9, a Cluster in next st) 3 times, (ch 9, a Cluster in 5th st of next lp) twice, ch 9, dtr in next tr, ch 9, sc in tip of point. Repeat from ** around.

EDGE—* 9 sc in next lp, (5 sc in next lp, ch 5, sl st in last sc for a p, and 5 sc in same lp) 9 times, 9 sc in next lp. Repeat from * around. Fasten off.

Stretch and pin right-side-down on a true circle 2″ larger than doily. Steam and press dry thru a cloth. Make a 2d doily.

LARGE DOILY—(19″)—Repeat thru Row 13. Make 4 more rows with lps 2 sts longer in each row (34-ch lps in Row 17). Repeat Row 14 of Small Doily with 30-ch lps,

Continued on next page

Star of Them All
Continued from page 92

Row 15 with 26-ch lps, Row 16 with 22-ch lps. Row 17 with 18-ch lps, next row with 14-ch lps, next row with 10-ch lps, next row with 5-ch lps, and a final row without lps between points. Repeat Lacy Points to *. Ch 5, dtr between next 2 Clusters on point, turn, (ch 9, a Cluster in 4th st between next 2 Clusters) twice, ch 9, a Cluster in 3d st of next lp, (ch 8, a Cluster in next st) 3 times, (Ch 9, a Cluster in 5th st of next lp) twice, ch 9, tr in next tr dtr between next 2 Clusters on point, ch 5, dtr between next 2 Clusters. Turn, (ch 9, a Cluster between next 2 Clusters) 3 times, ch 9, a Cluster in 3d st of next lp, (ch 8, a Cluster in next st) 3 times, (ch 9, a Cluster in next lp) 3 times, ch 9, tr in next tr, dtr between next 2 Clusters on point. Fasten off. Repeat between all points. Turn, join to one point, * ch 11, dtr in next tr, (ch 9, a Cluster between next 2 Clusters) 4 times, ch 9, a Cluster in 3d st of next lp, (ch 9, a Cluster in next st) 3 times, (ch 9, a Cluster in next lp) 4 times, ch 9, dtr in tr, ch 11, sc in point. Repeat from * around. EDGE—* 12 sc in next lp, (5 sc, a p and 5 sc in next lp) 13 times, 12 sc in next lp. Repeat from * around. Fasten off.

Stretch and pin right-side-down on a circle 3" larger. Steam and press dry thru a cloth.

Doily Drama
Continued from page 76

around, ch 2, 1 d c in each of the next 2 d c, 1 d c in next ch, ch 3, skip 1 s c, 1 s c in each of the next 5 s c, ch 3, skip 2 chs, 1 d c in next ch, join.

22nd Row. Ch 3, d c in next d c, * ch 2, d c in loop, ch 2, d c in same loop, ch 2, 1 d c in each of the next 3 d c, ch 3, skip 1 s c, 1 s c in each of the next 3 s c, ch 3, 1 d c in each of the next 3 d c, repeat from * all around.

23rd Row. Ch 3, d c in d c, * ch 2, d c in next loop, ch 2, d c in next loop, ch 2, d c in same loop, ch 2, d c in next loop, ch 2, 1 d c in each of the next 3 d c, ch 3, 1 s c in center s c, ch 3, 1 d c in each of the next 3 d c, repeat from * all around.

24th Row. Ch 3, d c in d c, ch 4, sl st in 3rd st for picot, ch 1, d c in next loop, * ch 4, sl st in 3rd st from hook for picot, ch 1, d c in next loop, repeat from * ch 4, sl st into 3rd st from hook for picot, ch 1, d c in same loop, * picot loop, d c in next loop, repeat from *, picot loop, 1 d c in each of the next 3 d c, skip the 3 ch loop, the s c and the next 3 ch loop, 1 d c in each of the next 3 d c, repeat all around.

Frost Fair
Continued from page 90

the 2 d c, 1 d c in next d c, repeat from * all around, ch 3, skip 1 loop, 4 s c in next loop, 1 s c in d c, 4 s c in next loop, ch 3, join.

20th Row. Ch 3, * 2 d c in next d c, 1 d c in next d c, ch 3, skip 1 s c, 1 s c in each of the next 7 s c, ch 3, 1 d c in next d c, repeat from * all around.

21st Row. Ch 3, d c in next d c, * ch 2, 1 d c in each of the next 2 d c, 1 d c in next ch, ch 3, skip 1 s c, 1 s c in each of the next 5 s c, ch 3, skip 2 chs, 1 d c in next ch, 1 d c in each of the next 2 d c, repeat from * all around, ch 2, 1 d c in each of the next 2 d c, 1 d c in next ch, ch 3, skip 1 s c, 1 s c in each of the next 5 s c, ch 3, skip 2 chs, 1 d c in next ch, join.

22nd Row. Ch 3, d c in next d c, * ch 2, d c in loop, ch 2, d c in same loop, ch 2, 1 d c in each of the next 3 d c, ch 3, skip 1 s c, 1 s c in each of the next 3 s c, ch 3, 1 d c in each of the next 3 d c, repeat from * all around.

23rd Row. Ch 3, d c in d c, * ch 2, d c in next loop, ch 2, d c in next loop, ch 2, d c in same loop, ch 2, d c in next loop, ch 2, 1 d c in each of the next 3 d c, ch 3, 1 s c in center s c, ch 3, 1 d c in each of the next 3 d c, repeat from * all around.

24th Row. Ch 3, d c in d c, ch 4, sl st in 3rd st for picot, ch 1, d c in next loop, * ch 4, sl st in 3rd st from hook for picot, ch 1, d c in next loop, repeat from *, ch 4, sl st into 3rd st from hook for picot, ch 1, d c in same loop, * picot loop, d c in next loop, repeat from *, picot loop, 1 d c in each of the next 3 d c, skip the 3 ch loop, the s c and the next 3 ch loop, 1 d c in each of the next 3 d c, repeat all around.

Monticello
Continued from page 91

next ch-4. Repeat from * around, ending with ch 5, d tr in 1st s c. **13th rnd:** Ch 11, s c in tip of next cluster, * ch 4, 3-d tr cluster under ch-5, ch 6, s c in next loop, ch 11, s c in tip of next cluster. Repeat from * around, ending with cluster, d tr in last d tr (at base of 1st ch-11) of previous rnd, s c under d tr-bar just made. **14th rnd:** Ch 17 (to count as d tr and ch-12), * d tr in next ch-11 loop, ch 12, d tr in loop following cluster, ch 12. Repeat from * around, ending with ch 8, tr in 5th st of ch-17. **15th rnd:** * Ch 8, s c in next loop, ch 6, s c in same loop. Repeat from * around, ending with ch 3, d c at base of 1st ch-8. **16th and 17th rnds:** * Ch 7, s c in next loop. Repeat from * around, ending with ch 3, tr in d c (at base of 1st ch-7). **18th rnd:** ** Ch 4, 3-tr cluster at base of ch-4, 3-tr cluster in center of next loop, ch 4, s c at base of last cluster made, * ch 8, s c in center of next loop.

Repeat from * twice. Then repeat from ** around, ending with ch 4, d tr at base of 1st ch-4. **19th rnd:** * Ch 4; in tip of cluster-group make 3-tr cluster, ch 4, s c at base of cluster, ch 4, 3-tr cluster in same place; ch 4, s c in next loop; (ch 8, s c in next loop) twice. Repeat from * around, ending with ch 4, d tr in d tr at base of 1st ch-4. **20th rnd:** * (Ch 9, s c in tip of next cluster) twice; (ch 9, s c in next ch-8 loop) twice. Repeat from * around, ending with ch 4, d tr at base of 1st ch-9. **21st rnd:** * Ch 9, s c in next loop. Repeat from * around, ending with ch 4, d tr at base of 1st ch-9. **22nd rnd:** Like 21st rnd, making ch-10 instead of ch-9, and ending with ch 5, d tr at base of 1st ch-10. **23rd rnd:** Make ch-11 loops around, ending with ch 6, d tr at base of 1st ch-11. **24th rnd:** * Ch 11, s c in center st of next ch-11, ch 4, 3-tr cluster in same st; 3-tr cluster in center st of next ch-11, ch 4, s c at base of last cluster; (ch 11, s c in center st of next ch-11) twice. Repeat from * around, ending with ch 6, d tr at base of 1st ch-11. **25th rnd:** * Ch 12, s c in next loop, ch 6. At tip of next cluster-group make 3-tr cluster; ch 4, s c at base of cluster, ch 4, 3-tr cluster in same place as last cluster, ch 6, s c in next loop, ch 12, s c in next loop. Repeat from * around, ending with ch 6, d tr at base of 1st ch-12. **26th rnd:** * Ch 12, s c in next loop, (ch 12, s c at tip of next cluster) twice; ch 12, s c in next loop. Repeat from * around, ending as before. **27th rnd:** * Ch 12, s c in next loop. Repeat from * around, ending with ch 6, tr tr at base of 1st loop. **28th rnd:** Like 27th rnd, making ch-13 loops (instead of ch-12). End with ch 13, sl st at base of 1st loop. Fasten off.

SMALL DOILIES (Make 2) ... Work as for large doily to 22nd rnd incl. Fasten off. Starch and block all pieces, stretching to measurements given at beginning of directions.

Glory

Continued from page 74

next shell, 1 d c in each of the next 2 d c, 5 d c over next loop, d c in next d c, d c in next ch 1 space, d c in next d c, 5 d c over next loop, d c in next d c, repeat from * all around ending to correspond, join in 3rd st of ch.

8th Round. Ch 3 and work 1 d c in each d c increasing 6 d c evenly spaced in round, join.

9th Round. Ch 8, skip 3 d c, d c in next d c, * ch 5, skip 3 d c, d c in next d c, repeat from * all around, ch 5, join in 3rd st of ch.

10th Round. Sl st into loop, ch 3, 1 d c, ch 2, 2 d c in same space, * ch 3, 1 d c, ch 1, 1 d c in next loop, ch 3, shell in next loop, repeat from * all around ending to correspond, ch 3, join.

11th and 12th Rounds. Sl st to center of shell, ch 3, 1 d c, ch 2, 2 d c in same space, * ch 3, 1 d c, ch 1, 1 d c in next ch 1 space, ch 3, shell in next shell, repeat from * all around ending each round to correspond, join.

13th Round. Same as 5th round.

14th Round. Same as 6th round.

15th Round. Same as 7th round but working 4 d c over each ch 5 loop.

16th Round. Ch 3, 1 d c in each d c decreasing 3 d c evenly spaced.

17th Round. Ch 3, 1 d c in each d c, join.

18th Round. Ch 3, 1 d c in each of the next 6 d c, * ch 5, skip 2 d c, 1 s c in each of the next 7 d c, ch 5, skip 2 d c, 1 d c in each of the next 7 d c, repeat from * all around ending to correspond, ch 5, join.

19th Round. Ch 4, d c in next d c, * ch 1, d c in next d c, repeat from * 4 times, * ch 5, skip 1 s c, 1 s c in each of the next 6 s c, ch 5, 1 d c in each of the next 7 d c with ch 1 between each d c, repeat from 1st * all around ending to correspond, ch 5, join.

20th Round. Same as last round but having 1 s c less in each s c section.

21st Round. Ch 5, d c in next d c, * ch 2, d c in next d c, repeat from * 4 times, * ch 5, skip 1 s c, 1 s c in each of the next 4 s c, ch 5, 1 d c in each of the next 7 d c with ch 2 between each d c, repeat from 1st * all around ending to correspond, ch 5, join.

22nd Round. Same as last round but having 1 less s c in each s c section.

23rd Round. Ch 6, d c in next d c, * ch 3, d c in next d c, repeat from * 4 times, * ch 5, skip 1 s c, 1 s c in each of the next 2 s c, ch 5, 1 d c in each of the next 7 d c with ch 3 between each d c, repeat from * all around ending to correspond, ch 5, join.

24th Round. Ch 7, and work same as last round but having ch 4 between each d c and 1 s c less in each s c section.

25th Round. Ch 8, d c in next d c, * ch 5, d c in next d c, repeat from * 4 times, * ch 2, 1 d c in each of the next 7 d c with ch 5 between each d c, repeat from * all around ending with ch 2, join in 3rd st of ch.

26th Round. Sl st to center of loop, * ch 6, sl st in 3rd st from hook for picot, ch 3, s c in next loop, repeat from * 4 times, ch 6, sl st in 3rd st from hook for picot, s c in next ch 2 loop, ch 6, sl st in 3rd st from hook for picot, s c in next loop, repeat from 1st * all around, join, cut thread.

Simple Crochet Stitches

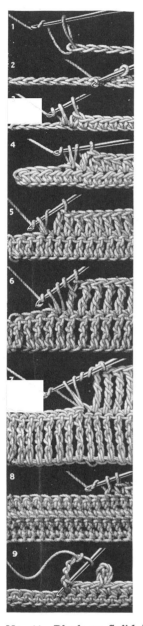

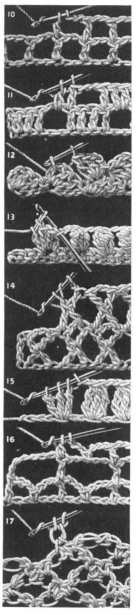

No. 1—Chain Stitch (CH) Form a loop on thread insert hook on loop and pull thread through tightening threads. Thread over hook and pull through last chain made. Continue chains for length desired.

No. 2—Slip Stitch (SL ST) Make a chain the desired length. Skip one chain, * insert hook in next chain, thread over hook and pull through stitch and loop on hook. Repeat from *. This stitch is used in joining and whenever an invisible stitch is required.

No. 3—Single Crochet (S C) Chain for desired length, skip 1 ch, * insert hook in next ch, thread over hook and pull through ch. There are now 2 loops on hook, thread over hook and pull through both loops, repeat from *. For succeeding rows of s c, ch 1, turn insert hook in top of next st taking up both threads and continue same as first row.

No. 4—Short Double Crochet (S D C) Ch for desired length thread over hook, insert hook in 3rd st from hook, draw thread through (3 loops on hook), thread over and draw through all three loops on hook. For succeeding rows, ch 2, turn.

No. 5—Double Crochet (D C) Ch for desired length, thread over hook, insert hook in 4th st from hook, draw thread through (3 loops on hook) thread over hook and pull through 2 loops thread over hook and pull through 2 loops. Succeeding rows, ch 3, turn and work next d c in 2nd d c of previous row. The ch 3 counts as 1 d c.

No. 6—Treble Crochet (TR C) Ch for desired length, thread over hook twice insert hook in 5th ch from hook draw thread through (4 loops on hook) thread over hook pull through 2 loops thread over, pull through 2 loops, thread over, pull through 2 loops. For succeeding rows ch 4, turn and work next tr c in 2nd tr c of previous row. The ch 4 counts as 1 tr c.

No. 7—Double Treble Crochet (D TR C) Ch for desired length thread over hook 3 times insert in 6th ch from hook (5 loops on hook) and work off 2 loops at a time same as tr c. For succeeding rows ch 5 turn and work next d tr c in 2nd d tr c of previous row. The ch 5 counts as 1 d tr c.

No. 8—Rib Stitch. Work this same as single crochet but insert hook in back loop of stitch only. This is sometimes called the slipper stitch.

No. 9—Picot (P) There are two methods of working the picot. (A) Work a single crochet in the foundation, ch 3 or 4 sts depending on the length of picot desired, sl st in top of s c made. (B) Work an s c, ch 3 or 4 for picot and s c in same space. Work as many single crochets between picots as desired.

No. 10—Open or Filet Mesh (O M.) When worked on a chain work the first d c in 8th ch from hook * ch 2, skip 2 sts, 1 d c in next st, repeat from *. Succeeding rows ch 5 to turn, d c in d c, ch 2, d c in next d c, repeat from *.

No. 11—Block or Solid Mesh (S M) Four double crochets form 1 solid mesh and 3 d c are required for each additional solid mesh. Open mesh and solid mesh are used in Filet Crochet.

No. 12—Slanting Shell St. Ch for desired length, work 2 d c in 4th st from hook, skip 3 sts, sl st in next st, * ch 3, 2 d c in same st with sl st, skip 3 sts, sl st in next st. Repeat from *. **2nd Row.** Ch 3, turn 2 d c in sl st, sl st in 3 ch loop of shell in previous row, * ch 3, 2 d c in same space, sl st in next shell, repeat from *.

No. 13—Bean or Pop Corn Stitch. Work 3 d c in same space, drop loop from hook insert hook in first d c made and draw loop through, ch 1 to tighten st.

No. 14—Cross Treble Crochet. Ch for desired length, thread over twice, insert in 5th st from hook * work off two loops, thread over, skip 2 sts, insert in next st and work off all loops on needle 2 at a time, ch 2, d c in center to complete cross. Thread over twice, insert in next st and repeat from *.

No. 15—Cluster Stitch. Work 3 or 4 tr c in same st always retaining the last loop of each tr c on needle, thread over and pull through all loops on needle.

No. 16—Lacet St. Ch for desired length, work 1 s c in 10th st from hook, ch 3 skip 2 sts, 1 d c in next st, * ch 3, skip 2 sts, 1 s c in next st, ch 3, skip 2 sts 1 d c in next st, repeat from * to end of row, 2nd row, d c in d c, ch 5 d c in next d c.

No. 17—Knot Stitch (Sometimes Called Lovers Knot St.) Ch for desired length, * draw a ¼ inch loop on hook, thread over and pull through ch, s c in single loop of st, draw another ¼ inch loop, s c into loop, skip 4 sts, s c in next st, repeat from *. To turn make ⅜" knots, * s c in loop at right of s c and s c in loop at left of s c of previous row, 2 knot sts and repeat from *.

Metric Conversion Chart

CONVERTING INCHES TO CENTIMETERS AND YARDS TO METERS

mm — millimeters   cm — centimeters   m — meters

INCHES INTO MILLIMETERS AND CENTIMETERS
(Slightly rounded off for convenience)

inches	mm	cm	inches	cm	inches	cm	inches	cm
1/8	3mm		5	12.5	21	53.5	38	96.5
1/4	6mm		5½	14	22	56	39	99
3/8	10mm	or 1cm	6	15	23	58.5	40	101.5
1/2	13mm	or 1.3cm	7	18	24	61	41	104
5/8	15mm	or 1.5cm	8	20.5	25	63.5	42	106.5
3/4	20mm	or 2cm	9	23	26	66	43	109
7/8	22mm	or 2.2cm	10	25.5	27	68.5	44	112
1	25mm	or 2.5cm	11	28	28	71	45	114.5
1¼	32mm	or 3.2cm	12	30.5	29	73.5	46	117
1½	38mm	or 3.8cm	13	33	30	76	47	119.5
1¾	45mm	or 4.5cm	14	35.5	31	79	48	122
2	50mm	or 5cm	15	38	32	81.5	49	124.5
2½	65mm	or 6.5cm	16	40.5	33	84	50	127
3	75mm	or 7.5cm	17	43	34	86.5		
3½	90mm	or 9cm	18	46	35	89		
4	100mm	or 10cm	19	48.5	36	91.5		
4½	115mm	or 11.5cm	20	51	37	94		

YARDS TO METERS
(Slightly rounded off for convenience)

yards	meters	yards	meters	yards	meters	yards	meters	yards	meters
1/8	0.15	2⅛	1.95	4⅛	3.80	6⅛	5.60	8⅛	7.45
1/4	0.25	2¼	2.10	4¼	3.90	6¼	5.75	8¼	7.55
3/8	0.35	2⅜	2.20	4⅜	4.00	6⅜	5.85	8⅜	7.70
1/2	0.50	2½	2.30	4½	4.15	6½	5.95	8½	7.80
5/8	0.60	2⅝	2.40	4⅝	4.25	6⅝	6.10	8⅝	7.90
3/4	0.70	2¾	2.55	4¾	4.35	6¾	6.20	8¾	8.00
7/8	0.80	2⅞	2.65	4⅞	4.50	6⅞	6.30	8⅞	8.15
1	0.95	3	2.75	5	4.60	7	6.40	9	8.25
1⅛	1.05	3⅛	2.90	5⅛	4.70	7⅛	6.55	9⅛	8.35
1¼	1.15	3¼	3.00	5¼	4.80	7¼	6.65	9¼	8.50
1⅜	1.30	3⅜	3.10	5⅜	4.95	7⅜	6.75	9⅜	8.60
1½	1.40	3½	3.20	5½	5.05	7½	6.90	9½	8.70
1⅝	1.50	3⅝	3.35	5⅝	5.15	7⅝	7.00	9⅝	8.80
1¾	1.60	3¾	3.45	5¾	5.30	7¾	7.10	9¾	8.95
1⅞	1.75	3⅞	3.55	5⅞	5.40	7⅞	7.20	9⅞	9.05
2	1.85	4	3.70	6	5.50	8	7.35	10	9.15

AVAILABLE FABRIC WIDTHS

25"	65cm	50"	127cm
27"	70cm	54"/56"	140cm
35"/36"	90cm	58"/60"	150cm
39"	100cm	68"/70"	175cm
44"/45"	115cm	72"	180cm
48"	122cm		

AVAILABLE ZIPPER LENGTHS

4"	10cm	10"	25cm	22"	55cm
5"	12cm	12"	30cm	24"	60cm
6"	15cm	14"	35cm	26"	65cm
7"	18cm	16"	40cm	28"	70cm
8"	20cm	18"	45cm	30"	75cm
9"	22cm	20"	50cm		